STORIES FROM THE

Bondi
LIFEGUARDS

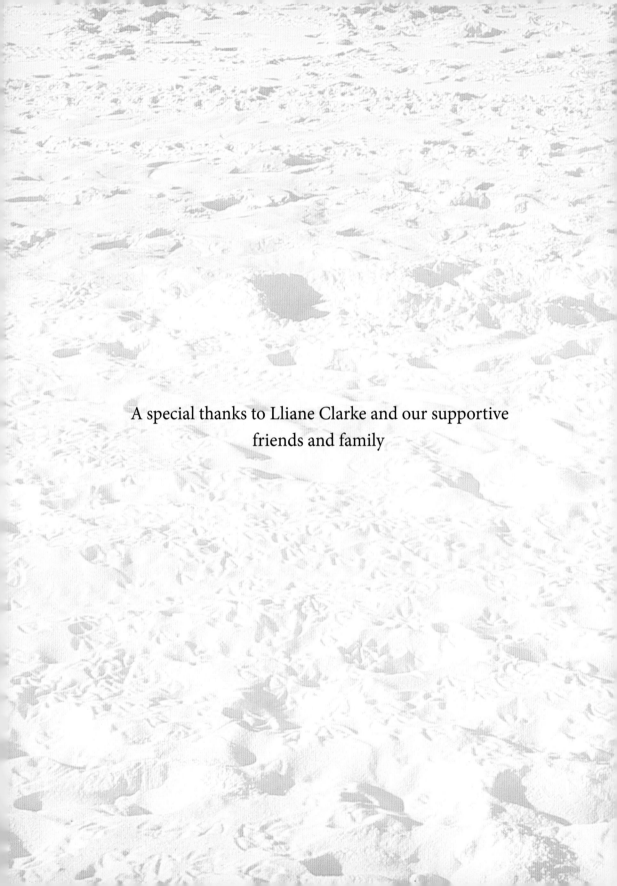

A special thanks to Lliane Clarke and our supportive friends and family

STORIES FROM THE

Bondi
LIFEGUARDS

BY

BRUCE 'HOPPO' HOPKINS • TRENT 'MAXI' MAXWELL • ANDREW 'REIDY' REID • ANTHONY 'HARRIES' CARROLL • ROD 'KERRBOX' KERR

NEW
HOLLAND

Contents

Introduction:

WELCOME TO SUMMER ON BONDI BEACH

LA has Santa Monica and Malibu, Hawaii has Lanikai and Waikiki, Rio has Copacabana, and Sydney has Bondi. Complete with a promenade that runs the full length of the beach, shops stocked with the latest beachwear, cafes and pubs serving everything from Mexican fajitas to the latest health food fad, Bondi is also party central. It's the place everyone goes to hang out – and where the world's celebrities like to be seen, mixing with the locals and going surfing.

Bondi also has our now famous lifeguards, the boys in blue who don't drive round in police cars, but take their rescue boards and 1800 horsepower jetskis out against the crashing waves of the Pacific Ocean to save lives – in all weathers, 365 days of the year. The Bondi lifeguards also work the beaches of Bondi, Tamarama and Bronte throughout the year, but it's only Bondi that has lifeguards on duty every single day.

The professional lifeguards are different to the volunteer lifesavers that operate on weekends and school holidays. That's not to say that the lifesavers are no less valuable! And their message to the public about water safety is crucial in the education of swimmers, particularly through their Nippers program for kids. But the lifeguards are professionals, trained in first response to any emergency.

Bondi is an icon of Australian history, its name in the Aboriginal language of the area means 'the noise of the water breaking over the rocks.' The original inhabitants were the Birrabirragal people who spoke the Sydney dialect of Dharug, and you can still see their artworks on the rocks on the north headland. It is now an icon of Australian history – it's where the first lifesavers started out, swimming against the breakers with a belt around their waist and a rope attached to a wheel on the beach.

Today the lifeguards put their own lives on the line to keep the beach a safe place. Their main task is to scan and spot people in the sea in trouble, before they get too far out of their depth, and bring them to shore as fast as they can. But that's not all they do. They are asked to deal with anything from a stubbed toe to a broken neck. They deal with homeless people, people passed out after a big night out, heat stroke, lost kids, people having heart attacks in the surf, people having epileptic fits, stings from blue bottles, family arguments, skateboard accidents.

All the action, and most of the decision making, comes from the central control tower, where Bruce 'Hoppo' Hopkins, the boss on the beach, is in charge.

Like all the Bondi lifeguards, Hoppo grew up in and around Bondi and the surrounding beaches. Local knowledge is a vital tool that the lifeguards have at Bondi. They know the way the rips and currents run, they know what the tides mean to the rock platforms out on the headlands, and they make the call of which way a swimmer or surfer should go to get out of trouble.

Bondi lifeguards work as a team and are great mates. There have been a few women who have taken up the challenge of being a lifeguard, and in the 2013 season Nicola Atherton started with the team, but mostly, it's a male dominated space in the tower. They are a competitive bunch when it comes to physical fitness. But they are also supportive of each other. Some of the guys have shared apartments with each other at various times, and they often go away together on tours or sporting events.

In the old days Bondi lifeguards had to prove their fitness over an 800m swim. Now to keep their job you have to prove it every year. If it takes over 13.5 minutes you have failed and you don't continue on the beach. So you have to bust a gut to get the job, and to stay in it.

Bondi is a south-facing beach, while most other Sydney beaches face east. Measuring about 1km long and 50–100m wide, it is among the widest of the beaches in Sydney. It is protected by two headlands, which form a neat cove or bay, to calm the waves before they hit the shore.

Bondi has what's called dependable surf – which means you can pretty much catch a wave there any time of the year. The waves roll in over a sandbank, and the north end of Bondi has a gentle surf perfect for bathing and general ocean fun! Surfing advice on the Surfspotsmap website describes it like this:

'Offshore winds blow from the north northwest with some shelter here from northeast winds. Windswells and groundswells in equal measure and the ideal swell direction is from the south. The beach breaks offer lefts and rights. Best around mid tide when the tide is rising. When the surf is up, crowds are likely. Hazards include rips, rocks, locals and sharks.'

'North Bondi is probably the safest beach you could have along the east coast,' says Hoppo. 'And even Bondi is a 'soft' wave. It's not the dangerous wave you have around Bronte and Tamarama, which the lifeguards look after as well.'

Bondi has a special history in the city of Sydney. It was one of the first places where the public could access the beach – and became a public beach in 1882. Two years later the government built a tram to get the Sydneysiders to the beach. It took 20 years for bathing in public to become legal there, and when it did, the Waverley Council built the first bathing sheds there in about 1894.

By 1929 an average of 60,000 people were visiting the beach on a summer weekend day. The opening of the famous Bondi pavilion that year attracted an estimated crowd of up to 200,000.

By the 1930s Bondi was attracting not only local visitors but also people from all over Australia and overseas. Advertising at the time referred to Bondi Beach as the 'Playground of the Pacific', a tag that has not been lost in the twenty-first century.

There used to be a sewerage outfall at North Bondi, which stopped a lot of the local Sydneysiders from swimming there, but now Sydney's treated sewerage is channelled out into the ocean several kilometres out, and the water on the shore is clean. This attracts schools of kingfish and snapper, as well as larger seagoing animals like seals, whales and sharks.

A TRADITION OF SAVING LIVES AT BONDI

As more and more people came to Sydney to swim on its famous beaches, like Manly on the north side of the Harbour, and Bondi on the southern side, there were increasing cases of drowning.

Professional lifeguards were first employed on the northern side of Sydney at Manly Beach in 1903. In response, the world's first formally documented surf lifesaving club, the Bondi Surf Bathers' Life Saving Club, was formed in 1907. Surf patrol members wore distinctive red and yellow quartered caps, which first appeared at Bondi that summer. Many key features of surf rescue were established in those early years, including several Australian inventions.

The club was responsible for introducing surf lifesaving to Australia and it pioneered the famous 'surf, reel and line', which gave the lifesavers (as they were called then) a connection on the shore to pull them back in. One early rescue in 1907 was one of a young boy by the name of Charlie Smith, who later went on to become the famous aviator Sir Charles Kingsford Smith.

The surf, reel and line system consisted of a belt around the waist of a guard connected to a winch on shore, which needed two men to operate it successfully. Hoppo has a funny story that he tells, about a lifeguard in the 1920s who was swimming out to rescue someone with their line trailing in the sea behind them. On the way, they passed a huge shark, which had been caught by a fisherman, being wound in on a line towards the shore.

The moment that thrust Bondi and surf lifesaving into the public arena was Sunday 6 February 1938. It was peak summer time and the city's population had headed to the beach. A large group of lifesavers were about to start a surf race when three freak waves hit the beach. Hundreds of swimmers were swept out to sea by a series of large waves and a flash rip, Bondi lifesaving club members performed over 250 rescues, but at the end of the day five lives had been lost and the occasion was forever etched into Australian history as Black Sunday. A similar event occurred in February 2005 where Bondi lifeguards were pulling swimmers from the sea as the amount of water

pulsing into the shore rapidly increased, and rushed out creating strong currents and rips in a short period of time.

'In fact someone has researched these two events and they reckon it was the same time of year and the same conditions,' says Hoppo. 'That's really weird. It's like we were facing the same thing that those guys were – same day, same time, same conditions, same area of the beach, all nearly identical.'

From Bondi, the surf lifesaving movement spread through New South Wales and then to the rest of Australia and beyond. With the reassuring presence of surf lifesavers on duty, beaches became places of secure fun, swimming and surfing. After World War II, surf carnivals, displays of pageantry, discipline, strength and skills, drew large crowds and even royal attention. A Royal Surf Carnival was held at Bondi Beach for Queen Elizabeth II during her 1954 tour of Australia.

Today, surf carnivals are big days in the beach calendar up and down the coast of Australia – when all the surf lifesaving clubs compete against each other for trophies. There's more women in the surf lifesaving movement now than there ever has been. So the image of heroic and brave men risking life and limb to save lives now includes women.

Bondi's volunteer lifesavers wear the traditional red and yellow. The Surf Life Saving Association volunteers patrol on weekends and public holidays during the summer months.

Lifeguards are the 'boys in blue' on Bondi Beach who patrol 365 days a year. The 35 Lifeguards are paid professionals employed by Waverley Council. They have ultimate responsibility for beach safety on Bondi and perform the majority of rescues.

Hoppo is proud of the service that he and others have built up at Bondi. He is always keen to show what happens behind the scenes in their daily lives, and what it takes to be a succcessful lifeguard. This book takes a look at the life of a lifeguard, and talks to five 'boys in blue': Trent 'Maxi' Maxwell, Andrew 'Reidy' Reid, Anthony 'Harries' Carroll, Rod 'Kerrbox' Kerr, Bruce 'Hoppo' Hopkins.

CHAPTER 1:

A talent for the ocean

A childhood growing up on the beach in Sydney is a pretty ideal way to start out in life – sun, sand, water, friends, ice-creams, exercise. It is also the best training you can possibly have if you want the job of a Bondi lifeguard.

All the Bondi lifeguards are local, they only had to ride a skateboard, walk with their parents, or catch a bus to get to the beach. Playing on the beach was just the beginning of what developed into a lifelong love of swimming, fitness and the ocean, which started early and has never left them.

Why is it so easy to fall in love with Bondi? Up the coast, north and south of Bondi, the beaches are stunning. From the endless sand stretching out across the Gold Coast and Surfers Paradise Beach in Queensland, to Byron Bay in New South Wales and down south to Bermagui and Bega – are hot beaches with peak surfing conditions. But Bondi, and its sister beaches Bronte and Tamarama, are unique; they are city beaches – situated right in the middle of a huge international metropolis.

Learning to swim in a swimming pool in a suburban backyard is one thing – but learning to swim in the ocean from a young age gives you a real sense of what it means when the tide is out or in, or what it feels like to be dumped on the sand after a big wave. The majority of the Bondi lifeguards grew up learning their water skills on these beaches, they know the tide patterns, good and bad times to swim and the places to avoid.

Growing up in Sydney means a summer spent at the beach, swimming in pools, hanging out with your friends in the local park. Water is a big part of life for kids in Sydney – they all want to get into it and play in it as soon as they can.

Learning to swim is not just how to do freestyle (it used to be called the Australian crawl or overarm) but about developing skills in personal survival and water safety. Getting out of your depth and being carried out to sea are the two big 'fear factors' when you're learning to swim.

Every kid in Australia is pushed to learn to swim. There are programs in schools, after school, and at holiday camps. In Australia we call little kids little 'nippers' and this name was given to a whole program for kids to learn how to swim and surf. It's called the Nippers program and it gives every kid from 5 to 13 the chance to go to school – on the beach!

Nippers is run by Surf Life Saving Australia, the organization of volunteers that started way back at Bondi. Some of the Bondi lifeguard boys started with that program, but they all wanted more than that – they wanted to be professionals.

First of all they had to learn how to swim – how to tread water and float on their back, how to dive under a wave and come up again. Confidently. Without these basic skills you will drown.

MAXI: 'I REALLY WANTED TO BE A FIREMAN.'

Trent 'Maxi' Maxwell grew up just down the coast, south of Bondi, at a place called Brighton Le Sands near Botany Bay. One of the youngest Bondi boys, he's been busting a gut to reach his peak ever since he joined at the age of 16.

Maxi wanted to be a firefighter ever since he was a little kid. He still thinks about the possibility of that in the back of his mind. It might have something to do with all his relatives who work in emergency services – his granddad was a paramedic and his brother was a firefighter.

'Oh and my cousin was a head parademic as well', adds Maxi quickly. 'So there are a fair few people in my family in the emergency services. When I was little I used to get so excited when I heard the sirens! We used to live near the main road, which was right near Rockdale

Fire Station. When I was three or four I used to have really good hearing. I could hear the sirens from miles away even while I was watching Teletubbies on TV and eating my vegemite sandwiches with no crusts! I would run screaming straight out of the front door to watch them go by.'

'If I was lucky I would get to the corner and catch the fire truck just as it was turning. If I was really lucky I would see two or three engines when it was a big call out, but that was really rare. I will never forget for my fifth birthday my uncle gave me some of his great firefighting stuff – a big hat and a jacket – and I thought it was the best thing ever. I got some overalls to match and as far as I was concerned that was it, I was a fully-fledged firefighter. I mean how many kids go to bed with their own personal fire plan! I would go to bed at night and I would put a hose nozzle and a spare piece of hose in the corner of the room. Right next to that would be my boots and a helmet standing by ready.'

'I will never forget the one time I went away with my cousins on a camping trip and a car caught fire right in our street – and the whole fire brigade were called to put it out right in front of our house! Massive engine fighting the fire! And I missed it! I was so obsessed with fire engines I perfected the sound that they make – I was really good at mimicking the siren. I could lean out of the car and make a real life siren and sometimes people would pull over in their cars! Well, let's say once they did until my Mum told me to pull my head in.'

Maxi and his mates grew up surfing at nearby Maroubra Beach, a 1km long beach with two surf clubs – North and South Maroubra. Maroubra Beach sits on the coast exposed to the Pacific Ocean and is surrounded by open space. It has huge pounding surf and deep water, and its name comes from an Aboriginal word for thunder – the sound of the surf on the beach.

Maroubra is not an easy beach to learn to swim on – it's great for experienced surfers who are confident in the water, but the likelihood of being dumped or churned up in the sea are pretty high for kids on their little boards.

'At school you could do surfing as a sport and that was my favourite school day! I loved surfing at school. Then I joined the club itself and became a member of the volunteer Surf Life Saving Club at South Maroubra. I went to school at Waverley College and then Marcellin College – I always went to school in the Eastern Suburbs. We did heaps of swimming at school and I also loved running – I was great at the cross-country competitions,' says Maxi.

'When I was a little kid I noticed these guys on the beach that weren't dressed in the orange and yellow outfits of the volunteers – they were the professionals. I saw them all the time. I had a relative that was a lifeguard and he was always chatting to me. I was so fascinated by their job and I could see that they were serious about what they did on the beach. I knew then I wanted to be a professional so I could do that work all the time. Imagine that! Being able to do it full time!'

REIDY: 'NOW MY LIFE IS AMAZING.'

Andrew 'Reidy' Reid was born and raised north of Bondi just up the hill, on the southern headland of Sydney Harbour in Vaucluse. Now it's an exclusive suburb, but back when Reidy was growing up there were lots of ordinary Australians living there. This champion Triathlete and Bondi lifeguard spent a lot of his early childhood on the beach and playing sport.

'I remember strongly loving the crystal clear water of north Bondi, the taste of salt water on my tongue as I caught the first wave of the day, the crispy feel of my sunburnt skin after a day at the beach – my nose used to peel like you wouldn't believe! I also remember the sound of the Mr Whippy ice cream truck pulling up in the north corner, and rushing up with whatever change we could get, only to have our ice creams melting as fast as we could eat them. We would spend all day out in the ocean on our little foam boards – we would stay for as long as we could, till it was time to go home.

'Every day we had to walk about 5 or 6km to Vaucluse Primary School where I went with my sisters. We would do it twice a day – there and back – every day! Mum made us all recite our times tables on the way to school as we walked along. She was really keen for us to walk to school and even on windy days or really cold days we would still walk. So off we would go – chanting as we went, five times three, five times four, five times five, etc, etc!'

'You can tell that my mum came from a navy background can't you!' Reidy laughs. 'Yeah actually my grandfather was the Rear Admiral of the Royal Australian Navy. It sounds like he was a pretty big man, and also tough on his kids. I got to meet him as a young kid – but I don't remember much about it, which is annoying because it sounds like he was amazing. Mum wanted to give us a stable life because she had travelled so much as a kid. They hardly spent more than six months in one place all over the world, as her dad kept getting different postings in different places all the time. She also had a really busy life travelling and seeing some amazing places as a kid. But she always said that she never had the same friends and she wanted us to have some of that stability. Dad was working hard selling cars and Mum worked hard too at jobs she could do and still look after us.'

'My parents got us all involved in the Surf Life Saving Australia stuff down at Bondi. My sisters were very talented swimmers and did a lot of competitions at school. We were always at the beach whenever we could go or at the harbor beaches, until I was about ten.'

'Then my parents bought a holiday cottage at a place called Lower Portland which wasn't far, but was inland north-west from Sydney. Every second weekend we would be there. We loved it. It had a huge river we could swim in all the time and one of the things we learned on the river was how to water ski – we did that a lot and we all became really good at it. We were quite a sporty family from an early age. I was regularly swimming in the training squad at Cranbrook Swimming Pool, and playing tennis at Rose Bay. My sisters were very sporty – competing in swimming and netball. My sisters (one older and one younger) were both such good swimmers they represented Australia at the Pan Pacific games. I liked swimming but I was never quite as fast as them – but I was fine with that!'

'One of the main issues that really bothered me as a kid was that I put on a lot of weight and became "the fat kid". When I was about 12, competing at school in swimming, I was friends with a kid whose mum used to send us down to the shop with $50 to buy lollies. Back in 1991 you could buy a massive amount of lollies for $50 – enough to fill a whole shopping bag – each! Most of the other kids were lucky to have $2.00. Cobbers, milk bottles, red skins, pineapple chunks and strawberries and cream I was a fan of them all. We would sit down in the park across the road from his house and just demolish a whole shopping bag each to ourselves then just lay there in a coma like state. We would eat this amount every day! Even though we had met at the swimming pool, we stopped going to the squad, stopped going to the beach.'

'Over a period of about 6–12 months I put on about 50 kilos, going from a fit looking little boy with a 6 pack to a slob with man boobs and a fat gut. I gave up sport and resorted to wearing baggy jeans and jumpers throughout my teenage years. I was chronically embarrassed to take my shirt off in public, I stopped doing the things I loved – swimming and surfing. And sadly I started smoking at 13. This was a habit that would be even harder to shake off than the weight. When I went to high school I went to Waverley College, an all boys school. So there I was the new kid, going into a single sex school where sport was pretty important, but I was the overweight teenager. Yes I got bullied even though there were a few other new kids. It was the overweight thing.'

'I'd stopped swimming as I didn't want to take my shirt off in front of everyone. I was really shy about it. The school had a reputation for really great swimmers and the teacher wanted me on the team because he knew that I could swim. But I didn't want to do that – I didn't want to get my gear off.'

'I think there's a fine line between bullying and being given a hard time and I don't justify bullying at all – but I don't think I would be where I'm today had I not been given that sort of tough love. I guess through that I learned how to toughen up. I took it – I didn't like it! But I took it. I guess all kids have different ways as to how they handle that and what they do with their lives later on.'

'The worst time was when we went away on a barbecue sleep over and there were games and activities. Girls from the local school also came along, I guess as we were from an all boys school they wanted us to learn how to relate. We were all around 16 years old and sitting around having fun. Somehow the talk got around to me, and everyone thought it was funny to make up a name for me. My nickname was Andrew Saggy-Arse-Double-Chin, I'll-have-another-leg-of-lamb, Reid. The name started small but by the end of the night it grew to this long name – I played along as much as I could, and tried to laugh it off, but it got to me and I got really upset. I wanted leave and my parents came and got me.'

'I mean kids are kids, and I think there is a way that you teach kids how to handle it. You do have to have thick skin. These days kids who are being bullied are not only copping it to their face but they are getting it all day on social media. And a lot of that cyber bullying is based on photos and images.'

'With their naval background my parents were pretty strict with us kids – and believe me we were never late to anything! We were always five minutes early! I don't think my parents would have let me have an iPad until I was 18 if they had been around in those days.'

'Because I was overweight and I was bullied I kind of alienated myself I guess and I tried to find a group of friends who would not hassle me and just treat me okay. So I found this group of a few guys and girls who weren't so sporty or active but they sort of accepted me so I fell in with them for a while. Two of the girls were having a hard time – they were copping a lot of crap at home and they wanted to run away. They were pretty young but as lots of young girls think, they thought if they ran away and got away from their parents it would all work out.'

'I thought of our holiday house, I knew that nobody was going to be there for a few weeks. I was genuinely trying to help them – I was young – that's my nature to try and help people. So I suggested they go there to our place at Lower Portland, and gave them my keys. They had to catch a train for two hours, and then get off and walk to the place, which would take them about four hours. So off they went into the middle of nowhere. Word got around Waverley College what was happening, and then it got around St Clare's, which is where they went, why they weren't at school. Next thing I know I get a call up into the Principal's office. "Okay tell us where the girls are, or we are going to expel you right now", the Principal said.'

'Well as you can imagine I told them straight away. The girls' parents and some of the teachers from the school got into a big car and drove there straight away. The girls meanwhile had finally reached the house after walking a long way to get there. There weren't any buses it was out in the bush! The hot water wasn't on in the house so they were boiling big pots of water to have a bath. Just as they were getting in the bath all the parents and teachers arrived! There were no mobile phones so I couldn't warn them with a text message or anything.'

'The principal came back to Waverley and said to me "Well we appreciate your honesty, and we are not going to expel you, but we do want you to leave." At that time I was having massive fights with my Mum and I was totally rebelling – I was a nightmare! I have spent every day of the last ten years making it up to her! Dad was working long hours selling cars, and Mum got another job driving disabled kids to school. She was under the pump and trying hard to make ends meet and she was really worried about me. So she said okay there is only one thing for you and that's boarding school! In Bathurst! Bathurst is a big town out west of Sydney – way beyond the Blue Mountains and very very far away from any ocean! I spent three days crying, saying "Please don't send me I don't want to go. I just wanted to stay". It was heavy. Mum said,

"Well too bad I'm doing this for you!" When she started to label all my clothes I knew she was serious!'

'When we got to Bathurst I said to her can I have a last cigarette before we go in? I was a smoker. So I got out of the car and ran into the field and hid. Mum waited in the office for two hours and I never went back in. After a time she got in the car and started to drive off – I came out of the field and ran up to the car. There was no way to get home from there otherwise!'

'I begged her: "Please please don't make me go there. So she said "Get in the car, you can go to Dover Heights School like your sisters". At that time the school had a bad reputation in the Eastern Suburbs and she was so upset, she just wanted me to be okay. So we drove back and I went to Dover Heights High.'

'Suddenly I was in such a different crowd at high school. It was all the kids in the Eastern Suburbs who couldn't afford to go to all the private schools there – there are a lot of private school kids in the Eastern Suburbs. The crowd there were kids from all sorts of backgrounds. There were boys and girls, big ones and thin ones, kids from all different countries, and everyone actually got on. There wasn't much bullying – just a great mix of kids. I ended up being in a school that I absolutely loved because I could just be myself! Now my mother is my hero – I thank her every day for never giving up on me!'

'All my new mates played sport – touch football, and basketball. So from 14–17 I was at this school that I liked. And we played sport! The local community youth centre had a basketball court down near Bondi and I used to go there a lot. It was a great centre and it really helped lots of kids get off the streets and into doing something worthwhile. As we got older we took the younger kids under our wings when they turned up there as well.'

'So I got to Year Ten in high school and Mum suggested that I leave and go get a trade, but no,

I was loving it – I had cool mates and was playing sport – why would I want to leave? I loved the school camps and meeting girls and we all got jobs at the local pizza shop so I had a bit of money as well. I passed my final year at high school – okay I wasn't the top of the school but I passed. It's so funny looking back because now I'm studying again and also pursuing a radio career. That's what growing up and being a lifeguard has done for me – because now my life is amazing!'

HARRIES: 'KIDS NEED TO GET OUT MORE.'

He's been called a spray tan advocate, a ladies man, and the *Daily Mail* in the UK can't write about him without referring to his 'hot beach body complete with a sizzling six pack.' Anthony 'Harries' Carroll is also a Triathlete and Ironman competitor, and generally what they call a natural board paddler.

Harries grew up in Clovelly, about 2km south of Bondi. Clovelly is a small inlet perfect for swimming, that sits between Bronte Beach and Bondi, and he gets his 'Harries' nickname from the name of a little surf break at Gordon's Bay in Clovelly. 'When I used to come over to Bronte as a kid they always used to ask me, "What's it like over at Harries?" I told them not to call me Harries.

'One of my earliest memories as a kid was in a running race at school. My mum was watching shouting me on but I came dead last in the race. What happened? She said I couldn't get my legs right! But it was probably also because I was a little bit tubby. I always wanted to win and wanted to be number one whatever I did. Well I have come second in the world in 2km running in the World Championships. So I got the legs right in the end Mum!'

'My parents both worked for Qantas. They both spoke several languages and had worked at the airline for a while. Previously, my dad was a sergeant in the army and was also a black belt Jujitsu. Then he got a job at Qantas doing corporate security, protecting the staff and the passengers. James Strong was the CEO there, at the time, and my old man used to travel around with him. Mum still has stickers around the house of the flying kangaroo!'

'Sport in general was something I adored as a kid but I wasn't that great at it,' says Harries. 'Football I was no good at, running I was terrible, swimming I was okay at. Did I fear the ocean? Absolutely! But surfing was the one sport that gave me all the happiness and it was something I wanted to keep going back to time and time again. I was addicted to surfing, I just wanted to do it whenever I could. And now I've won the Australian Longboard Championship title in the opens. Well I guess it's something where practice really does make perfect.'

'My twin brother Sean and I were both pretty hyperactive and to top that we had dyslexia. Surfing was a real outlet for us. My mum couldn't swim and she still can't really! She can only just float. Her mother was Egyptian and her father was Italian and when the war broke out they had to flee and they hopped on a ship and came to Australia. They love the beach, but they aren't great swimmers. But for me and my brother, the beach was everything. We got foam boards when we were nine and by the time we were ten we were surfing by ourselves at Bronte and Bondi and Coogee. We would walk or catch the bus to the beach whenever we could – after school, on weekends, whenever. It's not like today when kids get picked up and dropped off all the time! We were pretty street smart. My brother and I were members of the local Bronte Surf Life Saving Club. They had all these competitions for surfing and we used to enter them all the time. I was a little bit into fitness training then but not a whole heap. I did know I wanted to be number one at whatever I did! I knew that then and I still do now.'

'At high school we went to Marcelin College. We struggled with our reading and writing I have to admit but we had a lot of friends and were pretty popular. There were always ways around it – I adore spell check!'

'We walked everywhere, playing with our mates, making decisions about what the best thing is to do so we didn't get into trouble. We had our eyes wide open. I like to say it's like you have eyes on the side of your head and it's these ones that you need to keep awake – looking out for the things you don't expect to see. Yeah we made a lot of mistakes but that's what kids did, and it was how we learned. We weren't locked into our iPhone or iPad all day. Kids are different now. I've got a little boy and I really want him to walk or ride his bike to school.'

'My brother and I both went through to the end of school and finished at Year 12. Neither of us was ready to go out in the real world that's for sure! We got a bit more confidence and grew up. What then? Well I wanted to do a trade; that was what all my mates were doing, but in many ways I was still too young and not totally prepared for the real world.'

'In the park or down at the beach we had fun, like kids are supposed to do. They drink milk and get bigger and stronger and are not stuck in front of the TV all the time on a beautiful day. It's funny that you know? Actually I'm doing a lot of pilates now and we do a lot of correctional work to put people's backs straight and their bodies more upright. Our bodies are changing from being hunched over a computer or a desk all day. Primitive man had his chest out and his head back. He was ready to run and walk or pick up a log or a dead pig for that matter! Our society has made our bodies close up and shrink. We need to get out more!'

KERRBOX: BORN AND BRED ON THE BEACH

Rod 'Kerrbox' Kerr was born and bred at Bronte Beach and as a teenager became an elite waterman and World number 6 professional surfer. He has lived in Bronte all his life.

'I'm really fortunate to live in the house where my mother was born and grew up as well. It was one of the first houses at Bronte, and obviously my grandparents lived there also. The house is right on the water overlooking the beach. You couldn't get much better than that. The house went hand in hand with my career as a surfer and then later on as my career as a lifeguard.'

'Was I into sport at school? Well I was always, always into swimming that's for sure. But the boys will laugh and tell you that I'm one of the world's worst runners. Let's just say that I wasn't that good at athletics! But I can run fast for about 20m and I played a lot of football (rugby league) and I loved it. In fact at one point in my life it was a toss up for me to either become a professional surfer or a footballer. I even got offered a job with the Sydney Roosters. But I would have got bashed about a fair bit on the field because I'm small, so surfing seemed a better option for me.'

'I started surfing when I was about four years old. All we had to do was walk across the road and we were on the beach. I could guage how the surf and water was looking from my front window. My grandad and my father made me wait until I could swim six lengths of the Bronte pool before I was allowed to have a surfboard. That meant if I fell off I could save myself.'

'We didn't have boogie boards, we went straight to foamies (foam boards) and standing up surfing. My parents would take me to North Bondi because it was a much safer beach to learn to surf down there. Bronte beach is lovely for families, and it has the tiny train you can ride on and the lawns for picnics. But it's a short beach and the waves are often shore dumpers. Actually Bronte is a bit of a dangerous beach.'

'My grandad, Todger Taylor, used to be a lifeguard at Tamarama so I knew what life saving meant. And I knew how dangerous the surf was for people who couldn't swim as well. My dad was a fireman at Kings Cross Station, so I guess you could say that I come from a family of people involved in rescuing people! My mother used to work at Marcelin College in the front office so she was involved in educating and looking after people as well.'

'My parents always encouraged me with surfing, and my Mum, Coralie, was a top swimmer. And as I developed, the guys surfing out the back of the waves would always encourage you to prove yourself. The older guys would always be saying "come on you can take it on". Bronte is a pretty dangerous beach and it drilled into you not to have fear.'

Like many of the Bondi lifeguards, Kerrbox went to school at Marcelin College.

'My sister Cathy was the captain of her school, and she was also the dux of the school as well. Yep she used to do all my homework for me! She was four years older than me – and was quite handy to have around the joint! The teachers always knew that I was handing in work that wasn't mine. For years and years they kept asking me, "Who is doing your homework? We are going to get it out of you one of these days!" Then they used to give me a mark of about 3 out of ten, even though I knew all my answers were right.'

'When I was a kid I joined the Bronte Nippers, which taught me a lot of water skills and how to paddle on a board. I met this other kid at Nippers called Bruce Hopkins. He went to a different school to me but every weekend we would see each other down at the beach. As we grew up we'd hang out and see how each other got on in different competitions. I used to surf and he used to paddle ski. We ended up growing up together.'

'I won my first surfing event when I was 12 – the state championship. I was passionate about surfing and every opportunity I could get I was there at the beach. I wanted to keep competing, so my parents sacrificed a lot to let me travel to all the events around the country. They would travel with me, which was really important, and we went all over Australia to compete in the national titles. I wanted to see how far I could go.'

Bruce 'Hoppo' Hopkins also grew up at Bronte Beach. His mum and dad are still living in the same house that they have been in for 55 years. The boss of the Bondi Lifeguards, Hoppo is an Ironman and triathlete competitor.

'I've been going to the beach since I was about five years old. My parents were members of the Surf Life Saving Club at Bronte and were always involved in organizing events and life saving on the beach.'

'In 1974 my parents and the other volunteers started up the very first Nippers program. It was originally a bit of fun with the kids and running around on the beach, then it progressed from there to what it is now. Now it's a great introduction to kids to start to learn about the surf and how to swim in the ocean. Plus it gives them a chance to join some competitions, that was 40 years ago. Then every other club saw what a great program it was and started theirs.'

'I liked school but I really loved sport at school the most. I went to Waverley Public School and Dover Heights High. At school I was more of a runner than a swimmer. I won early teenage competitions when I was between 12 and 16, and I won the Australian titles in beach sprinting. I was really interested in getting into the sport rep teams at school – that meant I could get days off! My Dad, Aden, was born and bred in the country, in Crookwell, a country town near Goulbourn in the sheep belt of New South Wales. He was brought up with the philosophy that you don't show your emotions and you don't show your fear. Toughen up was his motto. He's 80 now.'

Hoppo's Dad had sport in his blood. He worked as a golf-club maker for Slazenger, was really into hockey and nearly got picked for an Olympic team. His mum, Joan, was a swimming coach and made a long-term career out of it.

'So my parents pushed me and my brother into sport and were always encouraging us to be active. Dad would come out with us in the water and help us swim a bit but he pushed me hard to do it myself. Looking back now I realize I wouldn't be doing this job if I hadn't been pushed hard by my parents.'

He's been described as "the quiet kid who was unsure of water." But Hoppo says that, 'It's a lie that you don't have any fear about big waves. I loved the beach but I have to admit that until I was about 11 or 12 I was petrified of the water and scared of the waves. I remember coming down the hill towards the beach and praying that there would be no waves and the ocean would be really flat for the Nippers session that day. Some days I really didn't want to go in the water at all. Everyone has their limits, especially when you're going into a situation where you do not know what's going to happen. I have a natural respect for the ocean. No matter how good you are at swimming or waterskills you have to realize that the ocean is a massively powerful force. Over at North Bondi you can see big rocks lying on the rock platform, basically 2 tons of rock that a big swell has just picked up and deposited up there. That's massive, and it shows you how dangerous it can be out there.'

CHAPTER 2

Why be a Lifeguard?

Somehow they were in the right place at the right time when someone suggested they try out to become a lifeguard at Bondi. For the guys (and a girl) who made it past the physical test into the job, it's changed their lives, and has turned out to be the best decision that they ever made.

Maxi jumped at the first chance he could get to become a lifeguard. Straight from school he was one of the youngest ever to be offered a casual job on the beach.

Kerrbox stands out as someone who had a stellar career on the beach before he joined Bondi Lifeguards. He was a champion waterman, ranking sixth in the World Championship as a pro surfer. Reidy had always loved surfing and was fit from working as a garbage man ('garbo') for Waverley Council. Harries and Hoppo were both fit athletes before they came to the job.

MAXI: 'THE BEST WEEK OF MY LIFE.'

Maxi's dream job changed as he got older from firefighting to working on the beach as a lifeguard.

'I had to find out how to make it happen! At first I went to Maroubra Beach and talked to a few people there, and someone suggested I go to Bondi to get a good idea of what's involved. So the next day I went to school and found my school careers teacher. I told him I really wanted to do work experience at Bondi and how could I make it happen. He said just write to them and ask! So he helped me write an email to the Bondi Lifeguards – it was addressed to Bruce Hopkins as the manager. I asked for a one-week work experience and that turned into one day a week while I was at school. Hoppo got back to me and said yes! I thought it was the best week of my life. I loved every minute of it. At that time I was about 15, in Year 10 at high school. A lot of my friends were leaving at the end of the year and like them I really wanted to start my career. There was no doubt in my mind where I wanted to be heading.'

'I have always gone 100 miles an hour at everything. I was always breaking things when I was a kid! But I'm different now. Being a lifeguard has changed all that. But I still go at anything with everything I've got. I guess I've also inherited from my family an ambition to help people out when they're in trouble. There's always been a sort of duty to the public in my family. When I first got involved at the volunteer surf club at Maroubra I could see that was part of my personality too. I got a taste of helping people and watching or helping out with rescues.'

'After my week experience down at Bondi, my career advisor suggested I asked if I could continue to volunteer every Monday. So I emailed Hoppo and asked him if I could do that and he said sure! Obviously I wasn't paid and I didn't even have my driver's licence – I had to get the bus and a train and a bus to get there. Who cares! I did that for a year until I finished my school certificate and was thinking of leaving school. The summer holidays began and in November Hoppo gave me a call and said they would like to put me on as a casual through the summer – working every Saturday. Wasn't I just loving life! I loved the responsibility and the whole group and I loved being one of the big guys, even though I was only 16.'

'By June the next year I was offered a traineeship and now I've been here at Bondi for seven years. If someone aged 16 started now working alongside with me I would probably think, "Oh my God, he is so young!" But I was really determined at that age. I wanted to be a really good lifeguard and I just fell in love with Bondi. The boys were very supportive and helpful –

guys like Kerrbox and Harries – they just embraced me as one of the team. It wasn't easy! Like it wasn't as if they didn't put me up for stuff all the time that was hard and really challenging. And it was hard to fit in with the older guys – I mean I was under the age for legal drinking so I couldn't go out and party with the guys and socialise. They weren't really my friends then on the job – I still had my school friends that I would hang out with when I wasn't working.'

'Then as I went through that first summer every Saturday as a casual, Hoppo told me they were starting a traineeship for two years and that they'd like me to apply. So that meant I would be working full time on the beach while going to college to follow sport and recreation courses.'

'Yeah I was on trainee wages, but that was fair enough I was young. You have to start somewhere – I didn't complain one bit. I would have done it for free I loved it so much! I learnt a lot about myself when I started the job. I realised that I'm not afraid to do anything. I do worry about some things – but I'm not afraid. One of the most important things I've learnt is how to balance things out. This job has taught me a lot about patience as well – there is a bit of down time when it's quiet and I have learnt to be patient. Wait, and watch you know?'

REIDY: 'WHY DON'T YOU HAVE A CRACK AT THE LIFEGUARDS?'

Reidy was working around Sydney doing the kinds of job young people do when they're checking out how it feels to be an adult. He was a smoker and had a weight problem but that never stopped him from giving 100 per cent to the job he had at hand. At 100 miles an hour.

'I was offered some work experience at one of Sydney's most famous seafood restaurants – Doyles at Watsons Bay, just north of Bondi. Doyles owner, Peter Doyle, has turned a humble fish and chip shop into a restaurant empire, an institution and international tourist attraction. It's a famous spot for tourists and in the summer is packed with day-trippers. Peter offered me a job as a kitchen hand. I was a local kid and he wanted to give me a start. Soon I was working in the bar, and it was really good fun, we had lots and lots of laughs! There was a large number of staff working there and we all had a great time and made lots of friends.'

'I've always loved an early start to the day. It's something I have always done. No matter how early – I'd much rather get up and go. So when I was offered a job in the deliveries part of the business I took it. Turning up for work at five really suited me! I could start at five in the morning and then have the rest of the day to go surfing. I have always loved surfing, it's always been in my life. What a life – working early and then hitting the beach!'

'The job was pretty hard. I was unloading all the trucks and then loading them up again, which was very physical work. We did two runs a day to deliver all the non-fish products. I started to lose some weight! Right, I decided, I don't want to be an overweight person anymore! So I just started eating differently. I would have a good breakfast, one sandwich for lunch and then whatever mum and dad cooked for me for dinner. I also started walking around the block in the evenings, and then I gradually increased that to a bit of a run and then I was running around a few blocks and it was getting easier to run further distances. The weight started to drop off!'

'Crunch time came, I remember, when I was out for New Year's Eve with all my friends and I really liked this girl. I wanted to kiss her and she said no! So I thought right, okay! And I dedicated the next year to losing more weight, increasing my exercise and not eating too much fast food. Not much more than that really, but it was enough to make a change. I was so glad to get rid of the weight. I really noticed a difference in my own body and understood more about fitness. I remembered that when I was a kid I really loved playing tennis and swimming and I wanted to get back into that. So I focused on it and spent that year getting fit and losing weight. And it worked!'

'Eventually I started seeing that same girl, and we dated for a while and then we both moved on. That's fine – I will always think of her as being my inspiration to become a healthier, slimmer and fitter person.'

'I was still a really good water skier, which I had learnt from all the time we had spent as kids at our holiday house on the river. My dad was one of the best skiers in the country. We did one ski, two skis, one hand, whatever. I kept up my skiing and surfing and with my weight going down I improved even more.'

'I saw an advertisement to teach waterskiing to kids at summer camps in America. I really wanted to travel, and I thought that would be a really good experience. So I applied and I got a job teaching waterskiing in the reservoirs and lakes in the Catskill Mountains in New York State. Boy did we have a good time! I've got some funny stories from then I can tell you! We had a ball! With six of my best mates we road-tripped down the East Coast of America and saw some amazing country. We had the time of our lives. I would love to go back.'

'For three years every summer I taught in America until about 2005. Part of the job was to supervise the lake with lifeguarding as well, so I had to do some qualifications like the American Red Cross certificate, CPR and First Aid. They put us through those courses and I passed them.'

'I still smoked but I thought I could counteract that with fitness. So I pushed myself harder in my fitness to see if I could keep up and not let the smoking affect me. Then a job came up as a garbage man for Waverley Council – I took it and I worked there for ten years. I worked on the hardest truck in the yard and it meant that I did a lot of running. There were guys on easy trucks who were overweight – so don't just think all garbos have to be fit! Some guys get an easier time of it!'

'What did I like about the garbo work? Yep, you guessed it, they started really early! And they finished early which suited me – it meant I could go surfing during the day at Bondi, which I loved.'

'All my friends knew I spent all of my spare time down at the beach. One of the guys at the garbos called Flopper could see I was into the beach. One day he said to me, "Mate why don't you have a crack at the lifeguards?"'

HARRIES: 'WELCOME ABOARD QANTAS, BUT NOT FOR LONG.'

'Ah the great outdoors,' says Harries. 'I've always loved it' And he doesn't mind some action in front of a camera either! A gig as the face of Australia's national airline Qantas took him right into the centre of celebrity. Checking out the lifeguards down at Bronte he decided to take a punt at that – a decision that's changed his life in many ways.

'When I left school I took up landscape gardening because it meant I was working outside! It seemed like the right thing to do. It was good fun and it kept me fit. I still love plants today and I loved working with my hands. I didn't mind getting dirty for a while then! I enjoyed it so much I even landscaped my own yard.'

'After about a year and a half, though, I had put on a bit of weight. We knew a lot of the lifeguards that worked on the beach and in 1996 I applied to the Council and got a part-time casual job. I did the swim test (I did about 11 minutes for the 800m), got my first aid certificate at St Johns, and started part-time shifts. It wasn't my whole life, though, I thought it would just be something I did every now and then, there was this general perception that lifeguarding wasn't a real career.'

'Because my parents both worked at Qantas I got a job there handling baggage to cover for the times I wasn't working on the beach, and I starting thinking about how to get into cabin work. One of my mates in the baggage section said Qantas was looking for someone good looking who could be the face of Qantas to promote their new business class Skybed. I said, "Mate, I'm going for that job!"'

'You know how it's all about who you know and not what you know? Well I got to meet the lady who was running the promotion and suggested myself as the ideal candidate… And I got it! Next thing I knew I was wearing a cabin crew uniform and travelling around as an international flight attendant wherever the Skybed went!'

'It was a fantastic job – I went to all sorts of promotional events and sat in all sorts of corporate boxes! I remember when the world cup rugby union football was on in Sydney at Homebush at the Olympic Stadium between the Australian Wallabies and the New Zealand All Blacks. Qantas had their own box, of course, and I was there with my friend who was a 400-metre champion runner.'

'I was in my international flight attendant uniform and we were having a nice time. Then suddenly Olympic gold medal athlete, Cathy Freeman walks in, and I was gobsmacked. Who would have thought I would be in this party with the Australian and Olympic champion sprinter right there, chatting and being really friendly? Cathy also introduced everyone to Joel Edgerton, her boyfriend at the time, an award-winning Australian actor who appeared in Star Wars.'

'Cathy didn't know I wasn't actually a flight attendant and that I was there as part of a promotional gig. Next thing she asks me if I could get her a drink? I look around and there are all these cups and glasses and I'm thinking oh hell what do I serve! So I had to admit it to her and say, look I'm not actually cabin crew, I'll have to ask someone else! We had a giggle and all sat down for dinner with the CEO of Qantas Geoff Dixon. Geoff knew my Dad as well.

I was chatting to Joel when he suddenly said, "Mate you rescued me at Tamarama!" He remembered me! Well that was a moment I can tell you. Never did I think that later there would be 160 countries watching Bondi Rescue on a TV series, and that I would be in a book!'

HOPPO: 'SOMEHOW THE BEACH WAS WHERE I WANTED TO BE.'

Hoppo hung in there at school and graduated in Year 12. His uncle was a reporter in the media and thought it might make a good career for Hoppo. So he pulled a few strings with some contacts in sports journalism, and before he knew it, Hoppo was down at one of Sydney's big popular commercial radio stations, 2GB. He worked there for four years. Not bad training for a guy who was later going to become an international television star!

'I started there as a trainee,' explains Hoppo. 'I got involved in the football (rugby league) round on the radio. Greg Hartley and Peter Peters were the football callers and they would need someone at the game to carry the mikes and the headphones. Then I would go and find whoever it was they wanted to interview. I'd be on the sidelines and then I would get the call and I'd jump up and grab the players when they came in, then they'd cross to the commentators' box and do the interview. I loved it – it was great fun because I could chat to all the players. I got to know blokes like Peter Sterling and Brett Kenny from the Parramatta team of the 1980s, then Laurie Daley and Ricky Stewart from the Canberra teams of the late 1980s/early 1990s and the Brisbane team with Langer and all those guys. It was a fun four years. Then Hartley and Peter moved on to another station. I was about 21, I was still learning and I wasn't in the box yet! I could see how cut-throat radio was as well. It was the era of major radio personalities like John Laws, Mike Carlton and Mike Tingle. I could see what I needed to do to get into the media. At the same time I was heavily into competitions, surf-ski paddling and Ironman racing competitions. I was competing and winning some state and Australian world titles, and having a great time. Somehow the beach was where I wanted to be, all the time.'

CHAPTER 3:

Surfing: the best training for a lifeguard

Rod 'Kerrbox' Kerr has the ocean running through his blood. 'When I was a kid, I just wanted to go surfing every day and I didn't want to go to school. I would get up every morning and then as soon as I came home I would go to the beach for hours and hours,' he remembers. Rod's parents could see where his passion lay and backed him to make a run at becoming a professional surfer. They knew it was going to be hard, as it costs a lot of money to travel and make sure he was in the right competition at the right time. But it paid off. For 10 years from age 17 to 27 his full-time job was to stay in the water and surf. It was the perfect training for what was to come.

SURFING: BIG IN AUSTRALIA, BIG ON BONDI

Surfing was officially brought to Australia in 1915 by Olympic swimming champion and early surfboard rider, Duke Paoa Kahanamoku from Hawaii, who demonstrated the ancient Hawaiian board riding technique on a board he brought with him, at Freshwater, on the northern beaches of Sydney. Duke Kahanamoku's board is now on display in the northeast end of the Freshwater Surf lifesaving club, and there is a huge sculpture of him riding a wave on the headland.

Duke gave surfing as a sport and recreation a huge push in Australia in that summer of

1914–1915. Already some Australian surfers were trying boards out and experimenting, but his contribution brought the mainstream media into the picture, and established some peak moments for the country's emerging surfing culture.

People along the coast of Australia became aware that surfing was part of an ancient tradition, and some even compared it to sports played at the ancient Greek Olympics. They also realised that it wasn't just on the beach at Waikiki that you could have a great time surfing – you could do it on the beaches of Sydney as well.

Duke didn't just do demos for the local people, he talked about knowledge of waves, and about safety in the surf and rescue techniques. He talked about surfboard construction and how the differences in design make such a big impact on the way the board and the rider can weave through the water.

But while Hawaiian surfers visited Australia lots of times, displaying their techniques on balsawood surfboards, the modern style of surfing in Australia came from California, during the 1956 Olympic Games, which Australia was hosting. And it came from the beaches of California where lifeguards were using boards to save lives. A group of Californian lifeguards were touring the east coast of Australia as a part of the Melbourne Olympic Games programme of events. They brought with them new lightweight 'Malibu' surfboards, taking them from Avalon on the northern beaches of New South Wales to Torquay Beach in Victoria. During the tour, an International Surf Life Saving Carnival was held at Torquay Beach. The competing countries included Great Britain, New Zealand, South Africa, Ceylon, and most significantly the Hawaiian and United States teams. The Hawaiian team was managed by surfing legend Duke Kahanamoku. This event crystallised surfer's interest and attitudes in Australia.

The Malibu boards that arrived in 1956 were highly advanced craft compared to the Australian racing boards, which had begun as a paddling board for Surf Life Saving Club events in 1934. Bob McTavish recalled 'I cannot convey to you what a sensation these little pods seemed to us… shock, delight, scepticism.'

Also in that crucial year of 1956, a local Bondi surfer and swimmer, Scott Dillon, was lent a balsa/fibreglass semi-gun with concave deck to surf at a Bondi Beach event organised by 'Flippy

Hoffman'. Also at this event, a mass performance by the riders showed off the long, sleek and tailored boards. A crowd of 50,000 people, and extensive press coverage, ensured the new Malibu boards were an instant sensation. Bondi's reputation as a glamorous place for surfing, was set in cement.

In a gesture of goodwill, the US & Hawaiian teams competed at more events at Avalon, Collaroy, Bondi, Maroubra and Manly over that 1956 summer. Their wave-riding performances created huge excitement in the beach crowds, an impact that was broadened when newsreel footage of the team surfing Collaroy was shown at cinemas. This was followed by a film entitled *Service in the Sun* (1957), commissioned by sponsors Qantas and Ampol Australia. The film, shot in colour rather than the usual black and white, included three and half minutes of the American team surfing at Bondi. After cinema release, the footage was shown independently in virtually every Surf Life Saving Club on the Australian coast.

The new surfboards used in these events remained in Australia, and were bought by upcoming Australian surfing identities such as Bob Evans (photographer and future editor of Surfing World magazine), Bob Pike (the first Australian International contest winner, in Peru, in 1962), and internationally renowned surfboard shaper Gordon Woods.

The 1960s was an important decade for surfing in Australia, and on the eastern beaches, surfing and surfers became cool, and admired. It was the era of the short board, and was the beginning of surfing heroes. The notes on the back of the 1962 album *Surfin' Safari*, by the famous Californian singing surfers, The Beach Boys, includes a tongue-in-cheek description of the sport of surfing:

'For those not familiar with the latest craze to invade the sun-drenched Pacific coast of Southern California, here is a definition of "surfing" – a water sport in which the participant stands on a floating slab of wood, resembling an ironing board in both size and shape, and attempts to remain perpendicular while being hurtled toward the shore at a rather frightening rate of speed on the crest of a huge wave (especially recommended for teenagers and all others without the slightest regard for either life or limb).'

Until the early 1960s the main activity down at the beach was body surfing. But with the new surfboards, and lots more money in their pockets than previous generations, the young teenagers of the 1960s travelled in their cars up and down the coast with their surfboards on the roof. The teen surfer subculture had begun.

The 1960s also saw the beginning of the journey to professional surfing, which Kerrbox became a big part of. This is typified now by the man they call the 'Michael Jordan of surfing' – Kelly Slater. But in Kerrbox's time, competition was just as fierce and it was just as hard to get ahead. His talent as a young kid was clear, and he rose fast through the ranks, riding every day on the beaches of Bondi and Bronte. Then he had to prove himself where it had all begun – in Hawaii, which has the biggest waves in the world.

'I probably had the most successful amateur surfing career to this date,' says Kerrbox. 'It's never been equaled. I won the state and Australian titles in my teens and was never defeated. In 1982, 1983 and 1985 I was the winner of the Quiksilver National Scholastics title and holder of the New South Wales title.'

Quiksilver is an iconic surfwear company that started out as a simple Australian board shorts brand. All the top surfers wore Quiksilver's cool board shorts and they quickly caught on. What was then a growing company now sponsors top surfers like Kelly Slater and major outdoor contests and events. It was Quiksilver that took Kerrbox on board and sent him to Hawaii to enter its competitions.

'I had some other sponsors as well,' says Kerrbox. 'Geoff Doig, a guy from Maroubra who was running a local surf shop, sent me off with some boards as well. I went to Hawaii on my own and I was only 15 – just me and my board and a lot of other top riders. I did have the option to knock the money back and stay as an amateur, but I was 17 years of age and leaving school, I had got backing from Ripcurl and Quiksilver, and I was off on my journey. As soon as you accept money you instantly become a professional. Bye bye football!'

'In those days, you could compete as a teenager in the professional surfing competitions –
now they wait till you're much older. They want to make sure you get the right breadth of
experience when you're younger. And I agree. I mean there are a lot of strains when you're
travelling around on your own when you're so young. You miss home, you can't rent a car and
you don't even have a credit card. So you have to rely on a lot of people. That was fine for me
because a lot of the guys did help me out. I had a lot of good friends and mentors.'

'Off we all went to Hawaii. I was living every kid's dream! I was really nervous as I was surfing
with the best in the world – but it was also very exciting at the same time. I wasn't scared of
the big surf there – growing up in Bronte you get used to big waves.'

'One day in Hawaii I was surfing a 25-foot wave at Waimea Bay. It was kind of scary and I had
a pretty good stack – I was under water and didn't come up for a few waves. I thought I was
going to die. My wetsuit got ripped off and my board snapped, and when I finally came up for
air I was in the middle of nowhere. I got to the shore and sat on the beach for about
40 minutes just shaking and shaking. I was terrified. That's what you have to do when you're a
young kid competing in amongst all these other big guys. I knew I just had to cop it and build
my own reputation. Then the other guys would look at me differently and maybe give me
some respect. I was starting at the bottom!'

'All the top professionals saw me fighting like that and they saw I was having a go. I knew
that if I couldn't prove myself in Hawaii then there wouldn't be much of a future for me as a
professional surfer. Hawaii is like the stomping ground and you have to go there and prove
yourself. I got through it!'

'For the next ten years I spent two months in Hawaii every year. There are three annual events
there – the Pipe Masters, the World Cup of Surfing and the Hawaiian Pro. If a surfer wins all
three events they are awarded the Vans Triple Crown of Surfing title, which is a professional

surfing milestone that rivals the Association of Surfing Professionals world champion title. I never achieved that but I did pretty well!'

'The Hawaiian competition starts in December when the big swells hit the islands. I made a few semis and quarter finals, which did get recognised by the Hawaiians. In the first year I travelled with Hawaiians, one of whom was John Shimooka. John and I went to the world amateur titles and were captains for our teams – me for Australia and him for Hawaii. We didn't like each other at first! We both had big egos! Then we bumped into each other at the bar, he gave me a bit of a nod and we had a beer and we were best mates after that! We travelled together for ten years – I actually introduced him to his wife.'

'Back in the 1990s, we certainly weren't regarded as athletes! Even though we were surfing every day for hours and hours, we were as often having fun, partying with bands and musicians hanging out with the surfing crowd such as Mötley Crüe, Public Enemy and even the guys from Sex Pistols. Some of the guys would bring their wives or girlfriends on tour. We always travelled on the same flights and stayed in the same hotels, like a big family.'

'John, Sunny Garcia, Derek Ho and I travelled a lot together. Derek won the World Championship in 1993 and Sunny went on to win the Triple Crown six times – more times than any other surfer in history. We were all young, hungry to win and pretty wild. I used to be called the white Hawaiian – it was a respect thing and I really appreciated it. Hawaii is where I get my nickname from – from the ex pro surfer Buzzy Kerrbox, who was a Hawaiian. We just thought that name was really funny, and it stuck with me!'

'Every year I would be away from Sydney for about nine months, surfing in about 50 events in that year. It was certainly a whirlwind tour. We went all over the world – Spain, Portugal, Brazil, France – the waves are really good in the south of France in places like Hossegor and Biarritz in the Bay of Biscay. Then we'd go to South Africa to Cape Town – there are really good waves there but the water is cold and there are lots of big sharks! We competed in surfing events all through Asia including four big competitions in Japan, which had lots of sponsors and competition money back then. I remember one surfing event in Japan that was held in a man-made wave pool! It was really fun. They had huge grandstands for everyone to watch and loud music blaring and people dancing – it was more of a party than a competition!'

'The problems for me were that I hated flying, (I still do!) and I hated being away from home for so long. I missed nine Christmasses in a row, that's how the guys all became like my second family, we just did so many things together while we were travelling so far away from home.'

'It's different now, there are only about 8–10 events and the guys can keep coming home in between. Also the top surfers now like Kelly Slater don't have to lug their boards around like we did. They are shipped over and are waiting for them when they arrive. I travelled with about 7 or 8 boards. I would pick them up from different manufacturers during the year – Gunter Ron was a shaper I used for a long time and he was my backer too. You have to have quite a few boards because they can break in the surf. We used normal short boards – ranging from about 5'10' to 6'. In Hawaii the boards were about 9'6' for the big waves and you had to have extra boards when you were competing in Hawaii because the waves are just so big.'

'One year in France I had all my boards stolen! I had two months there to compete in 8 events. I remember ringing home and just crying down the phone. We had gone out to dinner and when we came back all our stuff was stolen. But funnily enough that was the most successful European leg I ever had! All the boys helped, lending me their boards, and I ended up doing really well! I made the quarter finals and I said to my friend Martin Potter – he was the 1989 World Champion – "Mate you're not getting your board back! I'm keeping it!" He said, "That's fine, okay, you can have it." That's what it was like. I've gotta say that life as a pro surfer was a rollercoaster! One week you might be on top of the world and earning lots of prize money. You would be treating everybody and then the next week your mate might be looking after you because he was winning. We were fiercely competitive out in the surf, but as soon as the hooter blew we were back to being mates again.'

'When I was in my late 20s the world pro surfing circuit was completely changed, and the 100 competitor entry was cut back so that only the top 44 surfers in the world could compete. I made the cut in the first year and was in the elite crew for a couple of years. Although there were fewer events and the tour was well organized, I started to think about the possibility of doing other things. One year I didn't make it in, and that started me thinking. I thought to myself, well I've had a good run, enough is enough.'

'So in 1994 I was in that scary place with a good career behind me, but not many other skills, not knowing what I was going to do. I'm never one to lie around for long. I did some repping for a clothing company for a while and then the head lifeguard at Bondi suggested I give it a go. Suddenly my surfing skills were really valuable. My old mate Hoppo was in the lifeguards and I still loved being on the water. So I thought, well why not give it a go?'

CHAPTER 4

I'm working the beach!

Bondi is the busiest beach in Australia for lifeguards, with thousands of tourists who often have limited English and can't read the dangerous current signs. There is a strong rip at the most accessible part of the beach, and the famous sandbank is a potential spinal injury trap. It's also party central, and at Christmas and New Year thousands of young kids come to the beach to get wasted. Add in blue bottles, sunburn and don't forget the skateboard bowl as well. Get the picture?

All the lifeguards who have stayed working at Bondi are attracted to the beach by these very same reasons! No quiet beach for them, picking up the odd stray dog, all these guys love the high octane action on Australia's iconic beach.

It's not easy to get a job on Bondi, despite lots of people thinking it's an easy ride to a suntan. Since 2000 the professionalism of the lifeguards has been taken to a whole new level, one that puts them in a different class to the volunteer surf lifesavers.

The volunteer lifesavers fill a valuable job on the beach – and provide an extra set of eyes and ears down at the water's edge. They have their own entrance requirements to become part of that club. To become a professional lifeguard you have to go through a more rigorous set of tests. There are about 500 lifeguards in Australia, working all over the country on some of the busiest beaches. Bondi and the Gold Coast in Queensland are the busiest. In the Gold Coast there can be 100 lifeguards working at the same time during peak times.

Lifeguards have to pass the first aid tests and keep up all the training on all the equipment on the beach – jet skis, rhino ATVs, defibrillators – and they have to apply to become an employee of the Waverley Council, which requires, a Senior First Aid Certificate, an Advanced Resuscitation Certificate and a Defibrillator Operator's Certificate. You will also need a jet ski licence.

That's the first aid and emergency side of the job. Then there is the physical fitness required to complete a sometimes grueling nine-hour shift when you are constantly putting your own body under pressure. You have to be able to complete a 800m swim in under 13 minutes and an M circuit. The M shaped course is a combination swim, run with and without a board. You swim out round a can in the surf, back in for a run, back out for a swim through the surf, then another run. Then you do the whole thing again, this time carrying a board.

That's two 600m runs, two 600m surf swims, a 600m board paddle and a series of rescues. That's hard work if you're not a strong swimmer. It comes from Ironman training techniques and is necessary if you're ever involved in a mass rescue situation. And it isn't just a one off test, it's an annual physical test for everybody.

'You have to be able to rescue someone, bring them in, and potentially go and do it all over again,' says Hoppo. 'You might be doing that 10 times before you can stop.'

There are other skills that Hoppo says are an absolute necessity for any of the guys working on the beach. There's something that many of the lifeguards talk about as peripheral vision – an ability to see a situation developing before it gets critical. And the ability to see someone out of the corner of your eye, doing something that's not normal, that doesn't fit the pattern of the regular beachgoer.

When you're dealing with the potential of someone drowning, even a 10 second delay to react can be crucial. That can be the time it takes for an adult to gulp in five massive mouthfuls of salt water, or for a child to slip out of view under the waves.

Goof around, go surfing when you're meant to be rescuing, or put the service in a bad light and Hoppo will see you in the tower for a chat.

Maxi says people tend to forget that Bondi lifeguards also have responsibility for patroling Tamarama and Bronte Beaches. Jumping on a jetski to go around the headland to these neighbouring beaches is common. But despite this, Maxi says he is living his dream in his job at Bondi.

'I'm so happy to be at Bondi!' he says. 'Now I've been here for seven years, I have got to know everybody in the team really well. When I started I didn't have many friends but now all the guys are my friends. I can genuinely say that I really like everyone – they all have something special about them. I'm so lucky to be part of such a great team, and that I come to work every day in a job where I can talk to everyone – and just be a positive and happy person.'

Maxi's parents worry about him sometimes. The pressure of the job and the pace of it can sometimes be hard to take.

'My mum gets a bit worried about me sometimes but she's used to it now. Both my parents are very supportive.'

Maxi would love to be working full-time on the beach, but he has to wait a bit longer for that. He is a seasonal worker, which means for three months he has to find other work in the winter months, sometimes helping his Dad out, sometimes travelling. He still can't believe how lucky he was to become part of the lifeguards when he was so young. But it's a mark of his determination and strength of character that he got in at that time.

'If someone that age started working with us now, I know I would say "Oh my God, he is so young!" But I was really determined at that age. I wanted to be a better lifeguard and I just fell in love with Bondi. I guess if someone else came along like that then it would be the same! Hoppo has been a huge mentor for me here. He's also been a lifeguard all my life! Hey Hoppo!

If you're reading this remember that the month and year that you started lifeguarding was the month and year that I was born! My whole life you have been a lifeguard mate!'

REIDY: 'I COULD SWIM ALRIGHT.'

It was Reidy's mate Flopper who suggested he should have a crack at joining the lifeguards. That was it. He was in.

'I knew I could swim alright, so I applied and went to the physical test. I was pretty scared but I got in. I couldn't believe that I passed! Then I had an interview with a guy called Crackers, who doesn't work here anymore. I didn't have a lot of other experience in rescue work, even though I did have the USA experience, so I had to learn a lot of things as I went along on the job.'

'A lot of the older guys had been here for over ten years – Kerrbox, Corey Adams, Pine. I got a job as a casual lifeguard and was still working as a garbo and any time they needed me I never said no. I was always available in the early days – any shift I could get. I was really eager to learn. They all nicknamed me Superkeen. I mean going to the beach to go to work are you kidding me? I loved it.'

The main problem for Reidy that he had to tackle when he joined, was that he was still a smoker. 'I smoked until I was 32. Hiding it from all my lifeguard buddies was the hardest thing I have ever done. I hid it from them for about 6 years. The funny thing was that everyone would see me smoking at parties and wouldn't say anything, but they didn't know that I would also be smoking on lunch shifts, quickly having a shower and splashing around a bit of cologne to cover up the smell. Its still quite frowned upon now and its all changed since then.'

'It's not good for a lifeguard to be a smoker. You need to remain calm in high intense situations and you need to be able to go out in a big surf and stay under water for longer periods than normal. And if I'm running out of breath because I'm a smoker that's going to affect my ability to do my job.'

'I was training extra hard to try and counteract the bad effects of smoking. Doing the tests as we do as lifeguards, it's quite easy to look like I'm fitter than the other guys. I would run hard. On a regular day I was smoking about 10 a day. I always said I would quit when I reached 30 and so I tried to do that. My dad quit as well – and I could see that it had really benefitted him. It got to the point where I realized it was bringing me down and stopping me from doing a lot of things that I wanted to do. I was handling my fitness but I knew if I got to age 35 or 40 and was still trying to stay fit and smoking, I wouldn't be able to cope. When they say it rules your life it does. You're always thinking about when you could have the next cigarette.'

'I looked up a lady who does hypnotherapy. I paid a lot of money for sessions with her but what she has saved me since then in not spending it on cigarettes is incredible. She normally does hypnotherapy with people who are having problems in the bedroom but she took me on with my smoking. So I told her my whole story about when I was smoking as a kid and how I got hooked. She put me under for half and hour, then I went back the next day and she put me under for three hours then two days later she put me under again for an hour.'

'Then she gave me instructions, on paper, so that I could hypnotise myself, which made me realize that it is all in your mind! You have the power to change anything about yourself. You're telling yourself that you have cravings! I know hypnosis doesn't work for everyone, but if you want to give up smoking it's worth every penny. I haven't been sick once since I quit smoking. My life is so much better now and I wouldn't want to go back there.'

Harries knew a lot of the lifeguards who were working on the beach when he was a teenager. Being a local and a surfer, he was often talking to guys on the job, and looking back Harries realises he and his brother must have been really annoying, always fooling about and getting in the way. Despite that, something about the job sunk into the annoying 15 year old.

'I just thought, I want that job! I want that image! I want all that passion that they have about it! So after my work at Qantas, I applied to the Council in 1996 and did the swim test in about 11 minutes for the 800m. I still had to do all the prerequisites of the job – I got my First Aid Certificate at St Johns then I had to get my jet ski license. In fact I had to get it the next day! I had never ridden a jet ski. I had no idea but I was pretty confident I could do it. So I go down to the registration office, and I'm looking at a good looking woman across the counter and the old 007 charm kicks in. I got my licence the next day! Did I tell you that I'm married to the most stunning person in the world now?'

'The fact that I could surf and swim got me through – even though I still have a massive fear of the ocean. It's always so unpredictable, you never know what could happen one day to the next. I know I'm fitter than 90 per cent of lifeguards on the east coast of Australia so I'm comfortable with that. But that's not to say there isn't a fear of the unknown.'

'Lots of people ask me why I choose to work at Bondi and not at Maroubra where I had spent a fair amount time surfing. Well first of all I grew up with all the Maroubra boys and knew the lifeguards well. But I idolized the head lifeguard at Bondi, George Quigley – he was like the golfer Greg Norman's double! He had a great bunch of guys on his team and they always seemed really happy at work. They seemed larger than life, but there they were still helping people at the same time! Well why wouldn't you want come to a job like that?'

'The other thing I realized about Bondi Beach is how good the bikini is! In the old days the lifeguards had to measure skirts and tell people to cover up. There isn't any measuring of skirts like they did back in the day on these bikinis! I would like to say a big thank you out there to all the bikini designers! They came out with one called the Tiger Lily and I can tell you I felt like a sabre tooth tiger! Thank you! It's not good for my health! Oh and my wife's name is Emily.'

'This beach at Bondi is the best playground on earth – you can go surfing or swimming or running or paddling or snorkelling. It's got it all. I love Bronte Beach as well because it's close to my heart and it's great for families. But when you come over the hill here to Bondi something hits you! It's the same feeling you get as a kid when you arrive at a fun park. I see it every day when I come to work. The happiness on people's faces as they run onto the beach, especially in the summer. The problem is they more often than not run into a rip at the wrong end!'

KERRBOX: 'I USED TO THINK LIFEGUARDS WERE WAVE NAZIS.'

More than half of the lifeguards on the east coast of Australia come from the professional surfing circuits. Surfing is the perfect on the job training to be a lifeguard, it teaches you to have a sense of the water, the rips, currents and waves, see where it's best to swim and best to surf, and assess quickly when someone is in trouble. Formerly ranked 6 in the world, surfing champion Rod Kerr found himself on the beach looking for a job, after the rigorous travelling and competitions on the circuit.

'I used to think that lifeguards were beach police', laughs Kerrbox, 'We used to call them wave Nazis. We couldn't believe it when the waves were running really well and there was a good surf on the edge of the flags, they would kick us off. Now I understand what it's all about – and I have a lot of patience for the board riders because they help us out heaps. We couldn't do all we do without them.'

'But when I finished on the circuit, I wanted to do something different – and that was difficult. I didn't have any qualifications or a trade. I've already told you about my great school expertise! Where was my sister when I needed her! She couldn't get me a job this time!'

'I had a surf shop at Maroubra for a while with one of my best friends David Gyngell – he went on to be the boss of Channel Nine. I was always talking to him about what I would do, trying to figure out which direction to go in – I was never scared about rolling my sleeves up and doing some labouring and doing whatever I needed to do to get by.'

'Then I ran into George Quigly, boss of the lifeguards at Bondi at that time. He said why don't you come and work with us? I knew that the water stuff would be easy but I didn't know whether I could handle the first aid and the heart attacks or deaths. I needed to do it first to see if I was up to it. There wasn't much time for me to make up my mind! The test was coming up and I had three weeks to get everything I needed! So I put my head down to get it all completed. About 30 guys were applying for the positions and I was really fortunate to get one.'

'It's really funny because I love being busy and I love all the action with the crowds. And I appreciate the responsibility of the fact that we have all these people's lives in our hands. It's a part of my life now, but when I started I found the huge crowds a bit overwhelming. Now I love watching people from all walks of life having fun at the beach. I love seeing how much happiness they get from Bondi – they get a real good vibe and you can see that look of amazement when they first arrive because it is such a pretty place.'

'I like to feel that I belong here – I have surfed here all my life. It's a "close to my heart" kind of place and I feel proud to be from here – privileged to be such a part of it. When I'm away travelling and people ask me where I'm from, they know where I mean when I say Bondi. You get recognised with that tag. Bondi is one of the most iconic places in the world.'

HOPPO: 'AND WE ARE STILL HERE!'

Hoppo was heavily into Ironman competitions in 1991 and doing well, standing a good chance in swimming, running, ski paddling and board paddling. At the time there was a well-known cereal packet that always featured the Ironman champion on the back.

'I really looked up to those guys on the cereal packets then,' admits Hoppo. 'But it's funny because I've got more of a chance to be there now than I ever have!'

Lifeguarding gave Hoppo a perfect fit – time to train on the job and after work, and time to keep up the competitions. He managed to keep it all going for about five years.

'When I first started lifeguarding I thought I'd try it for about five years and then I'd probably move on. And Kerrbox was thinking the same thing. But we are both still here! That was because it wasn't treated as a profession – there was this tag about it just being a beach bum job. But there were still people needing rescues, even if there weren't as many, and not so many ski paddle and surf school kids in the water.'

'On my first day at work I was on a shift at Tamarama. I got handed a pair of shorts, a shirt, a whistle and a couple of badges to sew on later. The older blokes there gave me some good advice, like, "never let go of the rescue board!"'

CHAPTER 5:

Bondi: a big year of big events

Bondi has always been an arena for big events in Sydney, sporting, social and cultural. It's a place on the map for the city as it is the shortest distance to a surf beach from the CBD (Central Business District). Plus with its tourist identity, it always catches the media attention.

CHRISTMAS DAY

This is a massive day on the beach when tourists from all over the world flock to the beach and enjoy a hot and sun-filled Christmas with the locals. The beach attracts thousands of people from colder climates wanting to be photographed having Christmas in the sun – one without snow, or chestnuts roasting on open fires, or roast dinners. It is completely opposite to a British, Irish or Swedish Christmas – and these are the countries where some of the high number of young people backpacking through Australia come from. It's what they come to Bondi for – Christmas day with a Santa hat, barbecued prawns and bikinis. It all depends on the weather of course! Some Christmas Days in Sydney can be raining and stormy, but if the city throws up one of its classic perfect days then the beach will be heaving.

One year Reidy got into trouble on Christmas Day when he was off duty and went swimming with his mate, champion athlete Spot Anderson.

'Spot has about ten brothers and sisters,' explains Reidy, 'And they had all been given lilos for Christmas. Spot suggested we all go for a swim, and I said sure – didn't have much else to do. So we went down to Bondi and took the lilos and were just messing about and taking photos and stuff. It was a pretty bad day – the surf wasn't massive but it was solid. We were taking selfies and stuff. Suddenly some member of the public rings up and says someone is drowning down at Bondi! They thought we were putting our hands up – and they rang the police, 000! So then someone else rings the helicopter, and we look to the shore and Beardie is on his way paddling out to us! We said, "What are you doing out here?!" And he says, "Go in! The police are all on the beach!"'

'It's what happens sometimes when the public panic and ring in. We get that when people ring in saying they've seen sharks and it's just a seal – we get that a lot. The lifeguards could see that we were out there – they didn't know who we were – but they could see that we weren't in any trouble, but they had to investigate because someone from the public had called up.'

Hoppo gets lots of calls from the public about what they have seen on the beach.

'I get people ringing up convinced someone is drowning, but it's just the lobster pots from the fishermen, out near the rocks. I am looking and looking and I can't see anything! It looks like someone in a swimming cap bobbing up and down – but the public is convinced it's a swimmer!'

A lot has changed since the 1990s, when there were very few controls over what people did on the beach on Christmas Day.

'Back in the 1990s, people used to come down with slabs of beer and a ghetto blaster in the back of their big ute,' says Hoppo. 'They would park their trucks and fly a huge flag – Swedish maybe, or a Brazilian flag – so all the people who were from those countries could join them. The problem was that by 5 o'clock in the afternoon they were blind drunk, and then they would jump in the water. One year a guy came down selling Santa hats and everyone was buying them. In Backpackers Rip all we could see was a huge line of Santa hats with bodies underneath them going out. So we had to go out and start rescuing all these drunk Santas.'

'One year Hoppo had to put the shark alarm on just to get people out of the water. It was getting dark, and they were still going in the water. There were just too many people and there was no light left. It's dangerous to swim in the surf in the dark, because you can't see the waves coming at you, and you can't see which way the current is taking you either. Plus nobody else can see you if you are in difficulty. It's also dangerous for the lifeguards to be working at night. It takes about 10–15 minutes to complete one rescue, on average, if we are going to do rescues we have to be careful we are not also putting ourselves at risk. You might go out in the water when it's still light enough to see, but by the time you are coming back it's dark.'

'So the Council made the decision that we had to pull all that and police it more, and it set up a function in the pavillion so that we could control people more. And then alcohol was banned altogether on the beach in 2004.'

Banning alcohol meant that people thought twice about going in the water when they had a lot to drink. They stayed in the pub for a bit longer. It's certainly calmed things down a bit – if it was hot and busy we would be rescuing people at night until about 9pm because they were drinking and not realizing.

A recent case of a lifeguard in Newport Beach in Los Angeles, USA, illustrates the dangers that the lifeguards can face in big surf or treacherous conditions. Ben Carlson had gone into the 10-foot surf at around 5pm to help a man in distress. Carlson reached the swimmer, but a giant wave knocked them both under the water. The swimmer re-emerged and made it back to shore; Carlson did not.

NEW YEAR'S EVE

Every New Year's Eve is a big event at Bondi, with fireworks, DJs, bars, and stage shows. It becomes a spectacular playground for mostly young crowds, who mix and party with each other from around the world and all throughout Australia. The crowds can number up to 15,000 people. The year that ticked the world into the 21st century, 1999 into 2000, was huge at Bondi when the local council approved a massive dance party event at the beach, and despite the weather being overcast there were still hundreds of people still on the beach the next morning. Most of them were tired, happy and hungover.

Some of the Bondi lifeguards will also go out to party after a long summer day on the beach but they are always on standby to try and prevent tragedies and accidents on the beach. Staying often onto a later shift on New Years Eve the lifeguards get down to the beach early the next morning, putting up the flags and checking all the sleeping bodies on the beach.

The risks of dehydrating on a hot sunny morning from alcohol are real, and the lifeguards are also facing people swimming while intoxicated – not a great mixture at any time. The lifeguards have to ensure that the partying doesn't spill over into tragedy. Even though alcohol is banned on the beach at Bondi, the effects of people drinking too much are part of the daily life of the boys in blue.

'It's a controlled and ticketed event that's held here on New Year's Eve', explains Hoppo. 'Mostly people don't go into the water at night, but they come down for the sunrise on the first day of the year. And people in the city will come down as well. They finish up in the bars and clubs there and come back for the dawn down here.'

'On a nice clear day the people will arrive at 5am, so that's when we start too – normally we start at 6am. The main issues on New Year's Day is drug overdoses and alcohol. The main risk is that they get badly dehydrated – lying there in the sun with no water. So most of our work is actually on the sand rather than in the water on New Year's Day.'

AUSTRALIA DAY

Another important day on the beach is Australia Day, on 26 January. This marks the day Governor Philip raised the British flag in Sydney Harbour and declared it was a colony of Great Britain. It's a day Australians like to celebrate outdoors, celebrating the great life and identity of being Australian – having barbecues, watching fireworks, or doing the classic Australian thing – surfing. It's also a day when the Aboriginal Australians protest about the British, a day that they call 'invasion day', so there can be tension on the beaches, with gangs of guys asserting their identity as Australians running into fights with other gangs who they consider 'non Australians.' There have been clashes on the south coast beaches of Maroubra and Cronulla.

'Bondi is not that affected by that,' says Hoppo. 'There are few standoffs but not much. Actually its also in the school holidays that we get problems' says Reidy. 'Kids come from other areas in Sydney and they don't respect the beach – they leave all their rubbish sometimes and don't treat it like the locals. That's probably when we are more likely to get fights. That rubs local people up the wrong way. We also deal with a lot of complaints about girls being treated badly by young guys from more conservative cultures. They get verbally abused or spat on because they are wearing bikinis or clothes that in some societies are forbidden. And we get dragged into that because we have to manage those situations. We patrol around the area and call the police if necessary – we don't have to jump in and deal with the people ourselves.'

'It has to be really bad for us to close the beach,' says Hoppo. 'If we think things are getting out of control then we will pull the flags down and put up the beach closed sign, but that doesn't happen much at all.'

'We usually only close the beach if we can't control what's happening in the water. That will tend to be about the water, not about the sand. So if we need to get people out of the water we will close the beach. On Black Sunday 2005 when we had to rescue about 250 people, we had all our lifeguards in the water and only one person in the tower. That means you can't respond to any other situations. So we will use the shark alarm to bring everyone out of the water.'

CITY TO SURF

In August Bondi Beach is the finishing line of the city's annual City to Surf Marathon Run, one of the largest running events in the world, attracting over 80,000 runners with staggered starts and different time zones.

The City to Surf dominates the entire city, roads are closed, traffic is diverted, and everyone is encouraged to enter no matter who they are – charity runners, fun runners, family runners. There are also serious athletes who complete the 14km run from the central business district of Sydney at Hyde Park to Bondi Beach. These runners are competing for recognition nationally and internationally, and will go on to run in other world city events.

Bondi Beach is open as normal on the day of the City to Surf. Over the years, many of the Bondi lifeguards have also competed in this event. When the run finishes, there is no better way to cool off than in the ocean – the beach often building to thousands as the spectators as well as runners use the ocean to recover.

'We put an extra guy on duty for City to Surf', says Hoppo. 'After all, there are 83,000 entries and with the addition of all the support people, there will be about 100,000 people on the beach. Plus there are all these VIP tents with people enjoying corporate hospitality of various types. If it's going to be a nice day, the temperature at that time of the year is around 17°C in the water, and that means everyone will jump in, so we hope the water goes down to 15 or 16 as that means everyone gets out again!'

Hoppo has the fastest race time out of the lifeguards so far (but there is some debate about Bluey Graham's time when he was a lifeguard), and is holding the record at 48 minutes 52 seconds. All the other guys are battling to beat it. Reidy has run for the last ten years and his fastest time is 49 minutes 46 seconds.

'Anything under 50 minutes is pretty fast,' says Hoppo. 'Everyone's trying to beat my time, but I think Reidy is over the hill now!'

'The main issues at a big event like this is that if a swimming incident happens trying to get ambulance and medical services through the crowd can be very difficult. If there's a spinal injury then that poses a problem. One year we had to walk someone with a spinal injury all the way to Marks Park because we couldn't get the helicopter in.'

The race goes through Sydney, Waverley and Woollahra Councils and Hoppo's job is to talk to all the organisers in preparation of that. Their safety and risk officers and insurance officers are all involved – and they have the same fears.

'I have lots of meetings before the race with Fairfax, the police, ambulance service, rangers, different people from the three councils that the race is being run through. People think they just turn up and have a run. But it's one of the biggest running events in the world, and it takes a lot of planning.'

'We went through the same process with the Olympics as well – the biggest risk was a terrorist attack. It's an open area. How do you do a security check? Everyone is carrying a backpack when you think about it – so you can't inspect all of these backpacks, but we have had processes in place since the Olympics so we have the right procedures. In that situation we would play a role to help people move down, obviously with the cooperation of the police.'

'Yes it's a job about crowd control and we are a part of that.'

CHAPTER 6:

Changing of the guard – the year 2000

Hoppo and the team take Bondi's lifeguards to a whole new level

By 2000 Hoppo and his team had turned around the lifeguarding service to make it a more professional outfit. Waverley Council had to change the way the service was operating on the beach, and in the closing years of the 1990s Hoppo was under pressure to be the person to make that happen. 'It was the crunch moment,' Hoppo remembers. 'At the end of 1999 we had just lost a total of 150 years of lifeguarding experience when a lot of the senior lifeguards left the service at the same time, and the millennium celebrations were going to be one of the biggest events that Bondi has ever had.'

During the last few summers of the 1990s the crowds were getting bigger and bigger, and on a hot day the beach could be packed with 40,000 people, much more than in the early days of the century when you might have got around 10,000. The types of people that came to the beach had also fundamentally changed since the early days, with tourists that lacked any kind of swimming knowledge and many people travelling who had no or very little English.

In the year 2000, Sydney hosted the Olympic games, and the beach also became a world class venue for beach volleyball. Crowds of around 9,000 cheered on the competitors, including Australia's own gold medal hopefuls Natalie Cook and Kerri Pottharst. They battled it out on the golden sands of Bondi Beach in an atmosphere of one big party, with people dancing and cheering and making the whole beach one infectious sporting event.

'I might be a bit biased but I think the beach volleyball set the tone for the whole Olympics, because of its playful, dynamic and colourful nature'. Five-time Olympian medal winner Natalie Cook told *The Weekend Australian (26/6/2014)*. 'The music, the beach, you could sit in the sand with your shirt off and feel like you're at a concert. We had "Bondi Dave" whipping up the crowd, getting the Mexican wave going around and the slow wave – I haven't seen that at a venue since. Before the games, beach volleyball was the ticket people would either swap or give away, but when it started it became the hot ticket.'

KERRBOX: MY DREAM JOB FOR SURE

Rod 'Kerrbox' Kerr started working at Bondi in 1995.

Kerrbox says that the year 2000 was a massive one for the guys at Bondi, and not least was working around the 2000 Olympics event. Volleyball events had been run in all sorts of outdoor places – a forest in Georgia in 1996 for example. The rules require a sand court divided by a net. Bondi Beach was perfect.

Two compounds were built and the beach was separated into two areas. A massive temporary 10,000-seat stadium was built to host the tournament, together with a much smaller stadium, two warm-up courts, and three training courts. The lifeguards had to run two separate teams – one at the north end and one at the south end.

'The Olympics were mad!' remembers Kerrbox. 'For two weeks it was 28–30°C weather and flat surf – luckily we didn't have a lot of water work! But we were under the pump for that two weeks – the atmosphere was crazy! We were lucky enough to watch some of the events – everybody had wanted Bondi to be part of the Olympics, although local protestors had tried to stop the stadium being built, saying that the amount of traffic at Bondi was already too intense. But it went ahead and was an outstanding success.'

'Olympic Beach Volleyball has a colourful subculture of fans. There was "La Bola" a Brazilian cheerleader who got the crowd revved up. Everyone was clapping and cheering to the music and the exciting play. The fans were attired in shorts and Hawaiian-style shirts in their country's colours. Then Chelsea Clinton turned up to watch, which added a security dimension to the whole thing. Plus there were live TV cameras and reporters from all around the world there so we had to make sure that it went off without a hitch. We didn't have responsibility for the event but with the greater numbers of people there we had to make sure that the swimmers were protected.'

'The beach stayed open, and of course the lifeguards were on duty to protect the public. The beach was cut in half, so at certain tides they couldn't get along the beach on the rhino ATVs. The jet skis were kept busy in the hot weather.'

'Since 2000 the council has really got behind the professional lifeguard service and they have let us drive the progression and improvement in the workplace. Plus they have backed us in helping us to deliver the best service we can – which has meant of course getting better equipment. We are one of the leading lifeguarding services in the world and its partly because of all the equipment we now have – we've set a benchmark for the stuff we use, such as the top boards, buggies and the jet skis. They are the best we can get and we are supported by the manufacturers as well in making sure we get the latest updates.'

Despite all the stress, the tragedy of lost lives, and the intense commitment that the job requires, Kerrbox is certain that this job was his life's calling.

'This is definitely a dream job for me – something I can't imagine not doing – it was meant to be for me. We used to say we are only going to be here for five years but we are still here battling on.'

HOPPO: 'A REAL JOB?'

'When I first started working here at Bondi, lifeguarding was thought of as a job you did before you got a real job. It was a fill-in job, seasonal from September till April then you did something else. And most of the guys were being trained up and getting to know the ropes, and then leaving for what they saw as more stable careers. But lifeguards were still needed here in the winter. The number of tourists is still high because Sydney in the winter can be just like a European summer, with temperatures around 18–20°C and the water still warm.'

'I wanted the service to be and look more professional and give it more stability for the guys coming through. It needed to become a career for lifeguards all around Australia and overseas. We were losing guys who were really good at the job. I had trained them up to be brilliant but they wanted a career path. There's no way we could have had the TV cameras in then, in terms of the procedures around what we were doing and the little equipment we had.'

'I worked with Laurie at Waverley Council to bring in new procedures and reports.' Recalls Hoppo. 'We worked with other lifeguards in Wollongong and had other consultants on the Gold Coast of Queensland. It's taken us 14 years to get it to where it is now. And now Bondi is a real leader in the entire lifeguarding response field.'

'I also wanted to boost what the public perception was of lifeguards. I know the guys are actively watching and checking out the beach all the time, even if they are having a cup of coffee and talking to someone. But if the public see them chatting, they lose a bit of respect. So we had to change all that from a public viewpoint – things like respecting the uniform when you're wearing it, and watching what you do when you're out and about. That was very successful and we did achieve that – although you have to constantly work on that as well. Its' easy to get lazy and fall off that pedestal. We keep trying to bring new things in and new training sessions, like when the guys went to Hawaii to learn life saving techniques in the big surf.'

'We do performance assessments now as well, we're constantly checking on how everyone is keeping up. Everyone was initially really reluctant about it and nobody wanted to say what their weaknesses were. Because part of that assessment is to be honest about yourself. So we had to tell the guys where they were weak, because they didn't want to admit it themselves. But I thought of a different way of putting it. I mean everyone has a weakness. So I said – there is a bar to be set and everyone has to be above that bar. You should feel comfortable that you're already above that bar. But if you improve your weakness by 2–5 percent then the whole team will be lifted above that bar. I have to look at the whole team – it might fall apart in five years – I have to look at the bigger picture. It's not just about the individuals. We all have to keep up to the standard. I know that not everyone is cut out to be a lifeguard. But I want people who are working here to do whatever it takes to stay here, to do whatever they can to pass that test.'

REIDY: 'A REAL COMMITMENT TO SERVING THE PUBLIC.'

Reidy has been working at Bondi for 11 years, and has witnessed first hand the way things have changed.

'We are ten times more advanced since I started – I mean the show helped but it was moving on anyway. When I first started we had one not very powerful jet ski and one bike. We were running between rips to do rescues – now we have three bikes to cover 1km.'

'Money and exposure has helped that. So on a busy day we can have two jet skis in the water to prevent people from getting into trouble in the first place. And we can go out the back and check out boats. Plus we have more staff in the summer – and we have a trainee in the mornings, which really helps.'

'Why am I still here? Three things that I love about working at Bondi. I love the busyness of things here. I'd hate working on a quiet beach unless I have other things to do, but here there is always something going on. Same at Tamarama and Bronte, they are always busy.'

'I really like the mix of cultures. I like seeing so many different people – you see so much and I love seeing new things. And then it's the most beautiful place, even on a cloudy winter day.'

'I think working at Bondi is a bit like taking a long drive – say like driving from Sydney to the Gold Coast without stopping. At the end of your shift you're shattered. You know what to look for as you get older but you're still constantly looking, a bit like driving – you might be doing the same thing but you have to be physically and mentally alert the whole time.'

'For me the commitment to the public has come through from my upbringing – it's everything my parents instilled in me as a kid. And also I'm a late bloomer – anything I do, I do later! I spent the last ten years of my life partying a lot and being a big kid! I don't have much to show for that really! But now I'm growing up.'

CHAPTER 7

Danger: sharks and rips

What is the number one danger at Bondi Beach – rips or sharks? Most people would say the shark for sure? Rips are strong currents that rush away from the shore to deeper water. When waves break on the shore the water has to go somewhere, and that's what creates a rip current.

Rips are everywhere on Australian beaches. They're the prime reason people get into trouble and are the source of most of the rescues on Australian beaches. The problem with rips is not the danger of the current itself, but the sheer panic that swimmers get into when they get into one. So you could say that rips are not the number one danger, but panic is! Swimmers in a rip often try and turn around and swim against it and try and get back to the shore. When they're fighting breaking waves, rising panic, and gradually getting tired, they're on a losing wicket. More panic. A mouthful of salt water. Now the swimmer is in real danger of drowning.

But there is a big secret about rips that the lifeguards are always trying to teach everyone all the time. Relax. Float. Go with the flow. It will run out of steam itself and then you can swim back. Easy?

Another message that all the Bondi lifeguards keep repeating is to swim between the flags, where it's the safest place. How many times a day? Too many to count. It's part of the job.

Sharks? Well they're rare in comparison. There have been shark incidents and everyone remembers the year 2009 as one when the bull sharks were particularly active in Bondi and Sydney

Harbour. Sharks are something that every swimmer and lifeguard has on their mind when they go out into the deeper water.

But if you have to weigh up what's more dangerous, all the lifeguards would say the rips for sure.

MAXI: 'OH, SO NOW YOU NEED MY HELP!'

Maxi says that the most annoying thing is when he sees people putting their towels and bags right under the dangerous current sign, and then going in for a swim. '"You're an idiot mate!", I say! I love it when I say to them, hey it's dangerous to swim there pointing at Backpackers, but they still go in. Then you have to rescue them! "Oh so now you need my help," I feel like saying!'

'Our main job on the beach is to stop people from drowning. It's mostly the people who don't know how to swim and who don't read the dangerous current signs or can't read the signs. They have no idea about the rips. They just see the water and want to get into it.'

'Growing up in Australia we are constantly told about the dangers of the ocean and how it's important to swim between the flags because that's where there are no rips. But other nationalities don't get told that. They don't have surf in the places where they grew up. They often have no idea, which is why they freak out when it all goes wrong.'

'A lot of us grew up around here. They say you have to know this beach to work on it. Well I don't know about that. I have been around the beaches for nine years – okay some of the other beaches have a different direction for the swell and different sand. But I have learnt to understand this beach and the way it's right in the middle of the city makes a difference as well.'

'Sharks? I have never seen one in nine years – but I helped a guy who had his arm ripped off by a shark once. Other than that I have never seen one here, even in open water. I swam in one of Western Australia's iconic events, the HBF Rottnest Channel Swim a 19.7km open-water swim from Cottesloe Beach to Rottnest Island. I swam with Hoppo and we never saw any sharks. But it's their home so we are going into their place you know? It's like them coming on land and eating us when you think about it.'

REIDY: 'YOU'VE GOT MORE CHANCE OF BEING KILLED BY A COCONUT'.

Reidy says that what you learn at Bondi in one year as a lifeguard you would struggle to learn anywhere else up the east coast of Australia. It's just the sheer numbers of people coming to the beach and getting out of their depth really quickly that makes a lifeguard's job intense here. And Backpackers is where they tend to go.

'Rips are always around – it's the ocean and it's the seabed. Rips can form anywhere,' says Reidy. 'There's always a rip in each corner of the beach but it depends on how hard its pulling whether people get into trouble or not. Flash rips are the most dangerous. They were part of the notorious Black Sunday at Bondi in 1938. There's a whole myth that it was a collapsing sand bar, but it wasn't, it was a flash rip.'

'It was a really hot day in February and they had to rescue about 250 people. Five people drowned and it was a bad day for Bondi. There was just this huge set of waves rolling in and it knocked people off their feet. Finally a big set rolled in and then the water rushed back out really quickly, dragging people with it. There just was too much water. That's a flash rip.'

'Nearly everyone can float if they just lie on their back or just relax. Some people in diving trips can float for two days. If people just relax and float in a rip, nine times out of ten they will float back into shore. Instead of panicking, swim out a bit and then swim out of the rip sideways – it's okay you'll make it. Backpackers doesn't take you far out to sea. It's not like in

Indonesia where once I was working there and there was a guy 2km out in the Java Strait in a rip. A boat would have got to him two days later maybe if we hadn't seen him! We looked through the binos and couldn't believe someone was out that far. But it's not like that here.'

'So what about sharks? They're out there – I know they're there! But they don't bother me. I can go 3km out to sea without any worries. I've been paddling out in the ocean and they don't bother me. If I'm going to die from a shark attack, well I'll just accept that that is my time! I would rather die like that than being hit by a bus, but you have more chance of being killed by a coconut.'

HARRIES: 'LUCKY ME!'

Harries reckons that Backpackers has got something special in it that attracts people into the water. 'That rip is magnetic – they love it. They can't wait to get out of that aeroplane, jump into a taxi, hit the sand and get into that rip! I don't get angry because straight after I pull them out, there is someone else who is going to jump in straight after them. It doesn't matter who they are or where they're from. Everyone is always asking about sharks. Well I can say that sharks don't bother me. They have come up to me on my board when I was a few kilometers out in the ocean and just sniffed me like a dog. They didn't like the taste I guess! That's not to say that they are not around! They certainly are!'

In 2009 there were sharks around. It was the first attack at Bondi in over 80 years. A surfer from Dover Heights, Glenn, was paddling out in the water late in the evening – it's often the time that sharks are out looking for fish to feed on. He was out there with another guy, Mick, and about 20 other people. Next thing Mick saw a large tail fin thrashing around and the shark grabbed Glenn's arm.

'Glenn screamed "Shark!" and managed somehow to scramble back on his board, helped by other surfers. Mick got back to the beach and ran up to the skate bowls to find someone with a phone who could call for an ambulance. Looking back he could see a large amount of blood in the water, where people were helping Glenn out of the water. His left hand was almost completely severed, and his bicep was torn and bleeding. The next day the beach was deserted. A few of the lifeguards on jetskis told all the swimmers and anyone on the beach what had happened. The beach was closed.'

'It was a young great white shark that bit him. He came to the tower a few months later and showed us his injury and talked about what had happened. It was sad for him as he lost his hand. He still goes out surfing – which is amazing. Good on him and true honours to him I say.'

'It was the fifteenth time that summer that we had to clear the beach,' says Harries. 'A lot of us reckoned the shark had come so close to shore because the water was a lot warmer, and there were plenty of schools of fish coming into the bay. At the same time we also got the news that a diver had been mauled in Sydney Harbour by a bull shark. Then there was another incident when a helicopter was flying overhead and filmed a picture of a guy on a board in 2008 and there were all these fish around him and a shark in the middle there, and the surfer just had no idea! The shark just left him alone.'

KERRBOX: 'I HAVE A BAD HABIT OF SEEING SHARKS.'

If you get Kerrbox on the subject of rips and currents and how dangerous they are, he kind of chuckles. He explains that rips are a surfer's best friend. It's their highway out back straight to the waves. Surfers have such a different opinion about rips to swimmers – they treat them like roads. And if it's a fast one all the better, it gets you back out faster to catch more waves. It's this attitude, and the ability to accurately read the ocean that makes surfers some of the lifeguard's best mates.

'A surfer will always be conscious of the conditions on the beach,' says Kerrbox. 'And these can change from one hour to the next. Surfers can see when the tide changes and when the wind

changes and what that means in terms of rips and currents. They always track an increase in the swell as they're looking for the best waves to ride. All the guys are just watching the waves all day long. It just becomes a habit as you're so intrigued by the ocean.'

'A surfer will also help in a crisis – anyone nearby will always come and give you a hand. We might have two or three people that we need to rescue and a surfer will often volunteer to hold one of them for you while we take the others to shore and then come back for them. We can't be everywhere all the time. I've relied on surfers on plenty of occasions. I know myself as a surfer I did the same thing. Surfing and lifeguarding really go hand in hand.'

'We try to accommodate the surfers then when we are putting up the flags too, and looking for the best place to swim and the best waves. Telling the surfers to move is one of the hardest jobs for me – I sometimes give them an extra half hour if they ask!'

'Sharks on the other hand, well me and sharks don't go together. Yeah I have been surfing with sharks. I have had a lot of encounters with them. I have had at least a dozen near misses where they have come close to having a crack at me. I've steered a few off a couple of times while I've been out surfing. I've sat up on my board quick smart when I have seen one and they have veered off or chasing fish. I don't know why but I have this tendency to see sharks,' Kerrbox chuckles again. 'I also know that with sharks there is absolutely nothing we can do about them. There are nets out there, but they are just a deterrent, they won't stop them coming in.'

'I remember one time, Maxi and I were standing up on boards and paddling in Sydney Harbour and all of a sudden he face planted on the board. "I think I've hit a sandbank", he says! And I say, "There is no sandbank in the middle of the harbour mate! What are you doing?!" Turns out a shark had nudged him and it pushed him over on the board. "Pin it!" I said and we started paddling for our lives back to the shore.'

'In this job we are often travelling around the coast on the jet ski – going up to The Gap or round to Clovelly to help out, and we do tend to come across a few sharks further out. Yes, the beach has a net strung low across the sand across the bay to try and deter them, but it's the ocean – their habitat – they have a right to be there. Of course, if it's a great white we will get everyone out.'

'To try and cure me of the shark fear last year we did the great white shark dive in Port Lincoln in South Australia which is notorious for great whites. It was Hoppo's birthday – so Dean, Jesse, Maxi and me went along as well. They sent the film crew with us, and we had to get in the tank in Port Lincoln with these great whites. They were burleying (throwing in dead meat as bait to attract the sharks) off the side of the boat and then I remember Maxi shouting, "Shark!". We all kind of jumped and it was like this thing was in slow motion circling around the boat – and then the boat crew said, "Okay you've gotta get in the tank now and go down." It was like every instinct was telling me to stay in the boat! And my legs were like jelly. There was no way I was getting in there! I think I actually vomited while I was getting in the wetsuit I was so nervous. But I did it, and I'm so glad because it was one of the best things I've ever done.'

'Sharks react to vibrations and the guys were rattling the cages to attract them. I thought the shark could get into the cage because there is a hole in it but they can't. We had underwater cameras with us so we could film it. There you are, down in this deep blue water, and suddenly there is 16-foot great white, right up close to you, and because they bring the bait right up to the cages they smash into them. I think they tend to mistake people for turtles and seals, I mean we look like that. We're not their first choice on the menu, if we were they would just come and pick us up, but they don't. The chance of you actually being devoured by a shark is really small.'

DANGEROUS
CURRENTS

'People thought that experience with the sharks would have clammed my nerves about sharks now, but actually I reckon it's the opposite now I have seen them close up! Now I can see that there is something that big out there and they can swim easily into Bondi. Some scientists had these tracking devices on some great whites and tracked them from South Australia and up the coast, and one of them stopped for a while near Bondi. They go into Sydney Harbour as well, it was amazing to see the route that they take and how close they came. Still, it would never stop me from going surfing.'

'I'm going to Fiji in a few weeks to surf at Cloudbreak. It's one of the best surfing breaks in the world – just a few islands out in the ocean. You're taken there by boat and they drop you off in the ocean. You just hope sharks are not there and you're not on their radar. But it's always on your mind.'

'On the other hand, Hoppo is always saying that there are much more car accidents and drownings from people swimming in the wrong places than shark attacks. Since the movie Jaws everyone thinks that a great white is going to come to the beach and look for people to eat. But if that was the case, and sharks were man-eaters, then Bondi would be one of their best feeding grounds, and it's not, not one person has died from a shark attack in Bondi since 1937. The shark nets are just a straight piece of net suspended in the water between two bouys. A shark could get though it if it wants to, the net just interrupts its swimming pattern so it turns and keeps heading on up the coast.'

CHAPTER 8:

Resuss – Medical first response

Everything and anything can happen down at Bondi. People having fun, getting stung, kids getting lost, or someone facing a serious accident. It's all part of the daily job in the tower that the guys have had to learn as they go along. No college course is going to teach you this.

There's blood, EpiPens, ambulances and rescue helicopters. There's fires, car accidents, sunburn, thieves and emergency resuss. You have to have incredibly quick reactions and at the same time keep calm under pressure. It's a tough ask and one that the team meet day after day.

As well as accidents from people's inability to swim, or surf, Bondi in the summer also produces all types of natural dangers. Its famous sandbank, that lures the swimmers into deeper water thinking they can stand, can suddenly drop into deeper water. Then there's the Portuguese man-of-war, marine stingers that we call bluebottles. Their venomous stings inflict intense pain for about half an hour. They can also produce an anaphalactic shock, and other aggressive medical reactions in some people.

The lifeguard's job is to be first on the scene with an instant response – to fix people enough to get them to the paramedics who will then take over. Once a lifeguard has stopped the bleeding or got a patient breathing again or strapped them onto a spinal board they are handed over.

Funnily enough Reidy hates the sight of blood, which is unfortunate because in his job there's a lot of it, especially when kids are diving off the flat rock at the northern end of the beach. They come to the tower covered in gashes and scratches. And there's often blood spilt in the skate bowl behind the tower, which the guys also have responsibility for.

'Yeah get a bit faint when I see my own blood,' admits Reidy, 'And if there's lots of blood I have to take a step back – say if there's a massive cut on someone's arm. I have learnt to just take a minute and think about what I have to do and then I'm okay. Once I know what to do I just do it and deal with it professionally. I enjoy helping people but I would never want to be a paramedic. I like the mix of action and different things here – and it's not always about blood!' Reidy remembers when he first started, feeling overwhelmed about how hectic it was on the beach.

'One season we had about 12 major resuscitations – we got 12 people back from the dead. Another time there were three Irish doctors who were on holiday and going for a swim. A big thunderstorm had been building up during the day, one of those storms where you are just hoping it would hurry up and get it over with so we could all start breathing again.' Chappo told me this story, as I wasn't there at the time.

'The Irish guys were all coming out of the water at the same time. One of the guys came running out of the water with a board and the lightning just struck him, right there in front of us. His friends were all yelling at us while we were doing CPR but they finally shut up when they could see we knew what we were doing. We kept going with CPR for about 20 minutes, losing his pulse and then getting it back again. We changed around on rotation, CPR is quite physical and intense to keep up. It was incredible that he survived and we got him back!'

'In another resuss situation, we were called to a 20-year old girl who had gone out in four foot surf and it had hit her on top of the head. She was knocked out and lying face down in the water. She was there for four minutes before we got to her. It was big surf. We pulled her out of the water and up on the beach. With the defib we shocked her three times and we had her talking before the ambulance got there. She was one of the first people that they deliberately induced into a coma in order to slow everything down.'

The lifeguards are always concerned to hear about the progress of people that they have rescued and to find out what happened to them in the hospital. Reidy was happy to find out this woman was fine, especially as she went on to have three kids to look after. Reidy remembers one incident when they lost a man, and couldn't get him back. It really impacted on him at the time.

'I remember an Indian man who came to the beach. We learned afterwards that his name was Yondon Dungu and he was going to be the next brain surgeon at the famous Victor Chang Cardiac Resarch Institute in New South Wales – he had just been promoted, and his whole family had moved to Sydney to be with him.'

'I was working the rip down in the south corner, which is notorious for the famous Backpackers rip – the strong current that takes swimmers out of their depth and towards the rocks. Its what the surfboard riders call their highway – it's the quickest way they can get out the back to the bigger waves. I was making a lot of preventative announcements on the loud hailer that day to get people to go up to the flags at the other end. Bondi Beach is basically split into two, the north end for swimming, the south end for surfing. It's the way we have managed it forever and it seems to work the best.'

'Around 4pm I was scanning the water as we do all day. I remember seeing an Asian man walking out on the sand bank about 50m to the north. The reason he stood out was because he had Speedos on. Asian men that swim at Bondi don't usually wear Speedos, they are

usually fully clothed and that made me assume he could probably swim okay – although I still thought it best to keep an eye on him just in case. As I scanned back to Backpackers and then south corner in front of me I looked to where the Asian man in the Speedos was. He was now just out the back of the bank, then in the blink of an eye he just slipped off the bank and put his hand up for help. I quickly radioed the jet ski, knowing he could get to him a lot quicker, but he was racing out beyond the headland for another rescue at Tamarama. I realised he wasn't going to hear me even though I was screaming into the radio. I then radioed the tower and told the guy in Bondi central I was going in for a rescue and to keep an eye on him for me, because he didn't look like a great swimmer.'

'I jumped on my rescue board and started paddling out. There were lots of surfers around and they could see I was looking around for someone. I wasn't sure if someone had grabbed him and had taken him in. I was shouting out to everyone but nobody had seen him go under so I went back to the beach. We started calling out on the loud hailer and broadcasting asking if anyone was missing but no one came forward. We continued to look for him for another 45 minutes but came up with nothing. We couldn't put all our resources into the search as we still weren't sure if he was missing as no one had reported it. Plus we had another 40,000 people to keep safe.'

'About two hours later, at about 6pm, we were starting to pack up. A little Asian boy came up to me in the tower saying he couldn't find his dad. "Where was your Dad swimming?" I asked. He pointed to the sandbank. My heart sank. With a lump in my throat I told the senior lifeguard in the tower to call the helicopter, and I launched the jet ski with another lifeguard. I jumped into the water with a scuba mask and snorkel and searched the water for over 90 minutes. As other lifeguards got wind of the situation they came from other beaches to help out with the search. We couldn't find him. The helicopter was doing searches in the bay and we couldn't see anything. It's a lifeguard's worst nightmare and I was living it. Meanwhile his young son, two daughters and wife sat on the beach wondering what was going on. It was their first week in this country and her husband, their father had just disappeared. It was heart breaking. When asked by police "could he swim?" his wife replied, "No, no he couldn't swim".

'I came out of the water about 8pm, it was just about dark and I was nearly hypothermic. Some of the other lifeguards took over and resumed the search with the helicopter, but it was a lone surfer, sitting waiting for waves right in the corner, who spotted the body. He waved at the lifeguards on the jet ski and pointed down underneath him. The lifeguards pulled the lifeless body from the ocean and dragged it up the beach.'

'There was a rip in the back of the sandbank with weeds in it. I think he must have got stuck in the seaweed. The lifeguards tried to resuscitate him on the beach. They had to work on him in front of his family, which is always really distressing. His family couldn't do anything but stand and watch, wide-eyed with shock. The ambulance came down immediately, but pronounced him dead right there on the beach.'

'Yondon Dungu was 42 years old. He moved to Australia with his family to start a new life. The day he died was his birthday, and the first day the family had come to Bondi Beach. I felt to blame for a long time. What if I'd done things differently, could I have done more? I have played the situation over in my head a million times. I now do believe there isn't much more I could have done. He went so quickly and without a sound. We save so many people down at Bondi on a daily basis, and have such a good record down there that I think when we do eventually lose someone it really hits home. It was a harrowing day. I struggled with it for a while but I lived with a lot of tough love in my house, I guess, as a kid and it sort of helps me get over things. The boys came over to my house that night. Hoppo pointed out that we deal with these things and they do happen, on average we lose someone about every four years.'
'I went back to work the next day after the drowning incident and had a debrief with the guy who trains us for CPR but still it upset me. I talked to my mum about how shattered I felt. And she asked me if the guy was a good swimmer? And I said no, he couldn't swim. And she

said well, what was he doing swimming there then? And in a sense she is right. I mean people take their own life at risk when they go in the water and they can't swim.'

'The family asked us to his funeral and a few of us went. He was Mongolian and the family was really grateful to us – we raised some money for them; their main breadwinner was dead and they were suddenly alone in this foreign country.'

'About a month later I was working up near the promenade - I noticed a woman, a long way down the beach floating towards a pretty strong rip. I could tell she couldn't swim very well and began to jog towards her. None of the bikes had left the tower so the other guys hadn't seen her. Suddenly she went under. Between her and me was about a 500m soft sand sprint and a 100m paddle. I broke into a sprint, calling the tower on the radio while I was running. "I'm going in", I shouted, 'In front of the pavilion.' Tearing off all my gear as I went, I got on to the rescue board and paddled out there as quick as I could. I never once took my eye off her. When I got within 20m of her. I could see the look in her eyes as she took one last breath and went under. She had given up, was tired of struggling to keep her head above water, she was about to drown. I paddled like crazy over to where she was, dropped my arm down from the board and reefed her up by her hair. She came up coughing and spluttering then caught her breath and began to cry. I started to cry too. We do a lot of rescues every year. Many are preventative rescues; some are like this one and really close calls. But this one in particular really reminded me of why I do this job. That woman is alive today because of me. I think that rescue was a higher power helping me and saying its okay! You can rescue people!'

'Now I look at it like this – people go into the ocean who can't swim. I am a good lifeguard and we all do our very best to save everyone all the time.'

Back in the old days lifeguards relied on a piece of string to pull themselves back in. It's different now, it's a new world. But even with the technology it can still happen.

Harries says that a good lifeguard will be able to anticipate the situation before it happens and then go in to defuse and minimize. Move the flags or move the people to avoid the danger of drowning. Do it now and think later, is his motto. Even so, Harries acknowledges you can't always be in the right place at the right time. And even though they are constantly scouring the beach with binoculars from the tower, you can't always see the precise moment when someone initially gets into trouble.

'I try to calculate the risk of it as I'm assessing what people are doing', says Harries. 'Most people in the water have less than half of the ability that we all have and they don't know what they are doing.'

'Dealing with the public doesn't bother me. I know that they are in a strange situation. It's not until you see people die that it shocks you. I have seen people die in front of me who have not been able to be retrieved. And at the same time I have been lucky enough to bring people back to life. To see life being sucked out of them and you're their last chance for them, then to have dinner with their family celebrating their recovery, is incredible. When you bring them back it's the best feeling in the world. It must be what I imagine it's like to have a touch down in the Australian Football League.'

Harries clearly remembers his first shift at Bondi.

'On my second day at work I had my uniform all folded up and ready to go at home, and I was really honored to put it on. So I put it on and turned up on time! I sat there for five minutes sun tanning up and we looked out to sea and saw what I thought was a bloke, waving his

arms. So I paddled out and it was a woman who had swum about 1km out to sea and was trying to commit suicide.'

'There is a clinic off Bronte called Murray Street which deals with people who are depressed or injured, and this woman was being treated there. I paddled out and picked her up on the board. She told me she was trying to commit suicide but she was too good at swimming and it wasn't working, she used to be part of the American Olympic swim team! So I paddled her in but she had taken so many drugs she fell asleep on the board. On the beach the doctor was there from the clinic and ready to take her back, so it made me feel really good that I had got her back safely! You can never tell what people are going to do in the water. And everyone drowns differently. Kids drown really quietly because they don't even know they are going down!

'You know death and taxes are all a part of life? We are all going to die. The only thing that separates us from animals is that we have a conscience. If I can help people to stay around a bit longer so they can get home safely to their family, I have done my job.

Harries has also spent a fair amount of his time helping young kids to learn about the ocean and the surf. It's part of the work of the Nippers group with the Surf Life Savers on the beach. He remembers one incident when he was working with kids, and a particularly stubborn man was drowning – quietly – and refusing help.

'I had about 40 kids on the boards at Bronte', he remembers. 'I saw an elderly man struggling. I paddled out and he called out to me to leave him alone. He went further out and I could see he was getting more tired. It was winter and there were no lifeguards on the beach, it wasn't the high season. So I paddled out again and asked if I could give him a lift in. He said he was fine, so I went back to the kids.'

'He was then really struggling and I went out again. I called out to him and asked him how much money he had, and that he was taking the kids' training time so perhaps he'd like to send a donation to the kids surf club! Then he was going under – I grabbed him and dragged him across the board – and made him apologise to the kids for taking their time. What are you? I asked him. Why were you so stubborn? He said he was a company director. He just couldn't bear to admit he was wrong. He was so pig headed that he had bossed everyone around, but to me on the ocean floor he would have looked like all the other pebbles out there. And I hope that he has learnt something from that.'

'One other rescue that stands out to me happened on my day off. I was coming out of the gym and I could see there was trouble. Next minute I was running down to assist Harry Nightingale, Bobby Yaldwin and Mouse. Mouse had pulled a little girl out of the water and I was 100% sure it was a plastic bag that he was pulling up! She was so tiny, this two-year old Korean girl, and I watched him breathe life into her, using just two fingers to do CPR, and he brought her back to life. That broke me down and I started crying.'

'I had always seen what lifeguards did and had the fundamental skills from the surf life saving. But it wasn't until I started here when it was raw in front of me that I realized what they really did. And there you're touching the flesh of the deceased or seeing the family member really upset and cry in pain to see someone they love dying. And you have to bring that person back – and sometimes it works but sometimes it doesn't.'

'And you know not once have I ever been given a cape on like Superman you know? We wear these blue shirts, we don't wear capes! We are just human, we do our best, but we can't work miracles. All we can do is our best.'

'It's in my nature to help people – I have always had that. You couldn't be a lifeguard if you didn't have that in you. And all the boys here have that and are the same. Winning a major surfing event is one thing, but seeing the gratitude in someone's face after you come and rescue them – when they thought they were going to die, there's no comparison to any pay cheque or any trophy. You can't describe how good the feeling is. When you're out in the water and you're the only thing that can save their life it is really amazing. People are grateful because you have their life in their hands. It happens day after day. We are giving someone a chance to live again, to see the next day, have another Christmas, see their family or have another birthday. That happens time and time again.'

'That's the beauty of the job – it is never boring, it is never dull. One minute we are sitting and the next minute we are running or paddling like hell. Bronte is a family oriented beach, with a nice park and a rock pool and a little train – even though the surf is pretty dangerous most of the time. Then I drive over the hill to Bondi and my adrenelin starts and it's game on. As soon as you put your radio in your hand and you open the door of the tower anything could happen and that goes for the next ten hours.'

'Black Sunday, February 2005, when we did over 200 odd rescues was the hardest and most stressful day I've ever had. We were pulling out ten people at a time, and it was crazy – we didn't lose anyone though! I'd said to Harries and the boys at the beginning of the shift that it was going to be a quiet one, and by the end of the day we had broken the record on the number of rescues. They said I jinxed it!'

'We also have to cover Bronte and Tamarama. Tamarama is a very dangerous – it's mainly for local people or those who really know what they are doing. Just recently we had a guy washed onto the rocks from around Bronte and he sustained such serious injuries that he died.'

'Bluebottles (Portuguese man-of-war) can also give us some major problems on the beaches. In some cases people get into such a panic about the pain that they are experiencing from the stings they talk themselves into a serious situation. We always put signs up and warn people but people still go in the water, especially on a hot day. Their tentacles are metres long and they have these tiny but really powerful darts along them. They are really really painful if you get them on your skin. The best remedy is hot water to calm it all down, and then ice.'

'One rescue I remember is one I'd rather forget. It was Christmas Day about 2009 I think and Reidy and his mate went swimming in Backpackers, fooling around on blow up lilos, and people kept calling into the tower telling us there were people who needed rescuing. So I raced down to save them and I realised they were filming in the water and that it was Reidy wearing a Santa hat! Yeah I was spitting chips!'

HOPPO: 'GETTING THE SAFETY MESSAGE ACROSS.'

One of the main reasons that Hoppo wanted the TV show about the beach, was to try and get their safety message through to the public. Maybe when they come to the beach they will swim in the flags! Hoppo's commitment to his job and the way he turned the service around was one of the reasons he won the 2006 National Lifeguard of the Year Award at the Australian Professional Lifeguard Association Awards. Has the safety message got through? To a certain extent – but a lot of tourists still arrive at the beach and hit the first place they see – the dangerous end with Backpackers rip. They just get so excited – they forget about what the water is doing. But then again there are so many people on the beach when it's packed that there's a natural movement away from the flags. Hoppo remembers a lady in Darwin who wrote to him about a resuscitation.

'Her two year old son had fallen into a backyard pool in Darwin. She came running out and saw him lying on the bottom of the pool and he had stopped breathing. She pulled him out of the water and although she wasn't trained she started doing a basic form of resuscitation just working on instinct. When the paramedics arrived they took over, and she had done enough to keep some level of oxygen circulating, and they ended up getting the kid back to life. She said she only knew what to do because of watching our show. If the show was never there, she wouldn't have even had the faintest idea of what to do. I was also told about a four year old kid, who watched the show. He was swimming in a pool complex indoors and his little sister fell into the pool and he realized she was in trouble. He ran and grabbed the lifeguard – rather than run to his parents. And that saved her. He had learnt that from the show.'

'Paramedics have told me about times when they have gone to a backyard pool drowning and all the people are just standing around in a panic not knowing what do. They get there in about 5 minutes after the call but the drowned person is still just lying on the bottom of the pool. Panic takes over and nobody even thinks to pull them out of the water! I've seen that level of panic as well. People are just gripped by it and they don't move. But if they watch us on the TV and see us going through the steps they might do something, rather than doing nothing.'

'I remember one wife and husband I rescued in the rip together and you could see the fear in their eyes. They didn't know what was happening or if anyone was coming out for them but the survival instinct had kicked in, for him anyway. He had her by the shoulders and was standing on top of her! She was underneath. I got her out of there, she wasn't under for too long, about a minute. He didn't remember what he had done, but I doubt she was going to forget, she was probably ready to put in the divorce papers.'

Like most of the guys in the lifeguard tower, Hoppo always has a funny story to tell. 'Our standard rescue procedure is to put the person face forward on the board while we paddle at the back. This is so the board glides on the waves and we can get back to the shore quickly. The only thing is that girls don't like it. They hate getting on the board as it means their butts are right in our face. We think that's pretty funny.'

CHAPTER 9:

The team in the tower: stress at work

Any job that involves dealing with the public first-hand is stressful. You have to be professional at all times, and follow the right procedures. You have to be polite, considerate and sympathetic, even if the person can't speak English. When personal tragedy strikes you need to be understanding and considerate.

Harries talks about superman's cape – and why they haven't been issued with one. It's the stress that all emergency or first-response workers face – they strive to solve the problem, get the person out of danger, and fix the situation so that normality can prevail. But it doesn't always happen like that, and the lifeguards can find themselves in situations that are beyond their control. Not least because their workplace is the ocean – a powerful force that changes every day and every hour.

Mental and physical fitness are required. All the lifeguards have to be at peak fitness all the time to handle the pace. They have to be able to paddle right out the back of the waves to grab someone, or run down the beach to help another lifeguard. Mentally, if they have an issue they need to be brave enough to put up their hand as well.

Most of the lifeguards have grown up in the area and have known each other at school or in the Nippers or from just going surfing every weekend in the summer. It means that some of the guys have a history together and they know where they are coming from.

The guys help each other out after work as well – at the moment Hoppo is living with Reidy. Hoppo says that Reidy is the boss at home and he's the boss at work! Reidy says that when Hoppo is cooking spaghetti bolognese it looks like a mass murderer has been in the kitchen.

Hoppo and Kerrbox grew up together in Bronte. Some people might think that's something that would get in the way of a working relationship, but Kerrbox is quick to explain that it actually adds to it.

'I feel comfortable because I can tell him anything. I know that's really good, and we have been through a lot of stuff together. We know each other – the good and the bad. Well, I know I have to wind him up sometimes to get him going! But that's just him! I'm pretty out there and outspoken – I admit that,' says Kerrbox. 'Hoppo is more calculating and a bit more reserved than me. But when the clock comes round and our shift finishes I wouldn't want to hang out and have a beer with anyone else. That's when your friendship comes into play from when we were kids, its really valuable if you're going through a difficult time. And that's certainly been the case lately with both of us really. We support each other in family stuff, like my parents haven't been all that well lately and Hoppo has been helping me out with that.'

The boys go from the lowest of the lows when they lose someone, to the highest of the highs when they manage to bring someone back to life. It's a feeling that they all say you can't compare, and it makes their job worth every other minute of pain and stress. The lifeguards who are working at Bondi now are working with a well-oiled machine, something that has been revamped and reworked since 2000. Many of them don't realize the amount of changes that have had to be implemented to make sure that they can do their job to the best standards not only in Australia, but in the world.

As Kerrbox says, 'A lot of the guys come in now and it's like they've made it to the Grand

Final, without having to go through the times when we kept getting the wooden spoon! In the late 1990s, we were almost gone and now they have come onboard they are on television and are part of a winning team.'

How the team is organized depends on the day roster. Hoppo has the last say on who is doing what role that day. All the guys take turns to be on the main watch in the tower with the binoculars, directing the traffic of rhino ATVs and jet skis. As Reidy says:

'Well if you haven't been out on the beach for a while then you go out. If you have been out on the beach for a long time then it might be time for you to come in. It all depends. We are such a great team in that we work together really well. It's like when a resuss is happening everyone asks themselves what am I doing? Is there something that I should be doing? If there are three other guys already involved then it's probably your time to go and help out somewhere else.'

'It's the same if you're in the tower if you have been out on the beach then if you come in then the guys will probably just get up and walk out and get on with it,' says Kerrbox. 'It's great to have a lot of the young guys on the team', says Kerrbox. 'It shows up the other guys if they are being lazy. And Maxi is a good role model for other trainees coming through like Harrison. They can see how quick and dedicated Maxi is to the job. Now he can take a leading role over some of the other trainees. We had this one trainee called Taco and he didn't like it when Maxi was calling the shots and filling him in on what he was doing wrong.' says Kerrbox.

Maxi was about the second trainee in the lifeguards to work and study at the Technical and Further Education centre at the same time. It's proved to be a successful strategy and it means that Hoppo can get access to young and fit trainees to help out when they need it in the summer peak times.

MAXI: 'IF YOU'RE STRUGGLING IN A SITUATION THAT'S WHEN STUFF CAN GO WRONG.'

'I knew resuscitation was part of the job before I started, but I didn't realize that a big part of the job was dealing with the stress of other people's lives. All of us in the team have different ways of handling that. Yeah, we kind of have a bit of fun with it but then we are all serious.'

'We have to be at our physical peak most of the time and we train hard to maintain that fitness. I go running and surfing and to the gym every day because if you're struggling in a situation that's when stuff can go wrong. We all know that if we are tired we put our hand up and communicate it, then 99 times out of 100 things can be resolved. We don't come to work if we are sick either because you can't do the rescues.'

'Hoppo has been a big influence on me. I trust him that if he didn't think I could handle the spotlight of the show he wouldn't have put me in it. They were looking for personalities and situations – me because I was young, Kerrbox because he was a legend, Nicola this year because she was a girl. And it was a bit of extra stress on top of your work, but if Hop thought I could do it, well then I could do it!'

'God knows where my life would be now if I hadn't become a lifeguard. I am so lucky. A lot of my other friends are in different lives – I am glad I had this opportunity. I used to be working at MacDonalds and wondering what the hell I was going to do. I think sometimes while I was at work I would even forget how young I was at some stages. The guys would always support me. I was over in Europe with Hoppo and we had a great time. I remember Hoppo talking to my mum saying yes we will look after him – I think at the end of one night I was carrying Hoppo home!'

Reidy says that in some ways the longer you go on being a lifeguard, the more you realize how things can go wrong. And the pressure can build up when you know that you can be the difference between someone living and dying.

'After 11 years of watching the beach', he says, 'I have seen people die and some really bad things happen and it makes me realize how naïve I was, all those things I didn't really take any notice of and now I can see all the potential nightmares. But without that experience and information, I guess I wouldn't be stopping things from happening. I pull people out of the water much earlier than I used to. I would rather be on the beach and not in the tower. The guys in the tower are expected to notice everything. But then we are always interrupted – we are asked to talk to people or asked for photos, and it's a mistake to take our eyes off the water. There are so many curve balls being thrown at you – so much pressure. A friend from the Central Coast worked here for a year and he said he did more here in a year than in 20 years of his whole career.'

Being a lifeguard at Bondi has changed Reidy's life and turned it around completely.

'After I turned 30, I really changed', he admits. 'Giving up smoking made me realize that I can be in control of my life. I can just decide to do something and it's done. I met this wonderful girl about the same time who made me want to better myself. We fell madly in love and had a fantastic relationship. She is a great swimmer and really inspired me. She encouraged me to quit the garbos and chase my dream starting my own business. We're still really good friends now and I will always thank her for that belief in me.'

'I also entered the Molokai Channel Paddleboard Championships in Hawaii which is about 32 miles. I got in the top 50 in the City to Surf marathon run. I wouldn't have been doing that ten years ago that's for sure. I really like the competitions and I like to perform and get better. I like to be around a healthy atmosphere – I hang around with a totally different bunch of people now. It's not about losing my friends, it's about growing and becoming someone different. I have had a lot of different groups of people in my life as I go through the different stages. But that's growing up as a person – challenge yourself. I have always wanted to climb Everest and nothing is out of my realm now! I have also taken up photography – I really like taking shots of storms and cool shots of the ocean. I pack a lot into one day.'

HARRIES

The shifts at Bondi are nine hours. Harries says 'nine hours of work is extremely easy but nine hours of lust is extremely hard!'

'No but seriously, you need mates and people around you who understand your pain when you work here. I've been really lucky. For example, the first day I started work here I was involved in a major incident. A life saving rowing boat came up the beach and hit a guy and crushed his ribs. He was bleeding into his lungs. He was dying, but my training kicked in, I didn't panic and I was part of the team that helped him. And it made me realize well you know, believe in yourself. You might not be able to spell it but you can still do it!'

'You pick up on skills at work – techniques that you acquire. It's like martial arts and going in the army, its called peripheral vision and you don't miss a beat. Its what you learn here. Is it a glamorous job? Yes it is in a way. You're out there, you're on the front line, people are looking at you the whole time. Is it emotional? Very, at times. Is it stressful? You could have a coronary sometimes it's so stressful!'

'How to handle it? You can only do what's physically possible for you. You have pulled 10 people in and you might lose one. But if you give me the superman cape I can rescue them all! Then again I'm only human.'

'The young guys on the roster are constantly needing to prove themselves – they are the new kids on the block and it makes them dynamic and energized. It can ruffle a few old feathers but I like the fact that they keep me on my toes. They teach me a lot too – how to handle a person or a fan that keeps coming up and bothering me for example. They are great – consistently. I always get the best out of everyone – get everyone's biggest asset and put it all together and you have a great team. Like a great bike – get all the best parts and you have a real racer.'

Harries says that the competitive element in the team doesn't stop them supporting each other when it comes to the crunch.

'If someone is in pain they are a really good bunch of guys. They are like heroes – you know these guys are like Anzacs? All of them would pick up their mates from the trenches. And hey jealousy isn't a bad thing – but generally they are all great natured and they have so many good qualities. And yes they are like a bunch of schoolgirls in many ways as well! Trying to get attention!'

HOPPO

After 23 years in the job Hoppo still loves every minute of it.

'I still find this job really exciting – I get an adrenelin rush when there's a challenge and we achieve it. I hate being in a comfort zone – I like being out of it and testing myself. I get bored easily! That's why I'm glad the TV show has come along and it's been a great challenge for me. I can tie in the business world and the media world while still being a lifeguard.'

It's Hoppo's job to make sure that the team is in peak shape. The last 14 years have seen him build a mean machine, ready for whatever is next. It's his job to see that weaknesses are addressed, any training provided to cover any gaps, and that there is a balance in the team between old and young, experienced and inexperienced.

Hoppo remembers Harries when he was a young troublesome teenager.

'I was working on the beach when Harries and his brother Sean used to come down here to Bondi. They used to hang around a lot at Clovelly and they would drive me nuts. They would always be up to something and causing mayhem. Running around, and surfing in the flags, stuff like that.'

'Then six years later, suddenly Harries decides he wanted to be a lifeguard. All the pranks and hard work he put on me, now he wanted to be in the job! And all those pranks haven't really stopped I don't think! Well he's settled down a bit now. I've known him for 20 years. I think bringing Maxi in was a good idea. At first I thougt he was going to be too young but he's worked out well. A few other guys persuaded me to give him a go – so I did. Probably under sufferance!'

'I think I wouldn't put anyone on now who was under 18. It wasn't until he got to 18 that he started to really function. I think 16 is too young. The job needs more maturity, physically and mentally. He has handled it well, though, and probably proved us wrong in some ways.'

'At the end of the day you want the guys to stay on, after they have been trained and after they have learnt what this job is about. I want to get about 15 years from the guys – I don't want to

go back to what I saw in the 1990s when the guys were moving on after a year or so as they only saw it as a seasonal job. We are all getting older as well and we are all going to move on as well. You want someone who has put the work in – you don't want that to fall apart.'

Hoppo is also keeping a look out for who will take over from him in the future to keep the standards up that he has worked so hard to maintain.

'I do a lot of talks to corporate companies about team management. When I listen to them they often talk about praising the people who are excellent. They keep talking about their strengths but their teams are never going to be any good if they don't pick up their weaknesses.'

'It's the same with a football team. You can't get your best players running around doing everything and leaving out the weaker ones – the opposition will always cover your best players and then you're left with the weaker ones, exposed. You need to bring up the weaker players to be on par.'

'This is just what I have learnt in practice. I have spent quite a bit of time with Richard Branson– I've taken him out on the jet ski and talked about a lot of things. He is similar to me. He didn't shine at school and yet he has a real vision. What I picked up from Branson was that he said to himself, okay we are running an airline. He picked the best people he could find to run it for him as he acknowledges that he can't do it himself. Then that person needs to be successful so he gets the next lot of people underneath him that he needs. That makes sense to me. That is the theory I put in place here and also in my business. If you're a self made person like Richard Branson or John Singleton, Australia's equivalent entrepreneur, you need people with the right education and skills you need – then you get them to work for you. That's how you're successful – you find the right people. You don't need a lot of university degrees to get that.'

'It's about team building. We have areas we can improve on for sure and everyone has their own ideas – but I think leaders are born not bred – and if you want to have a team that is the best and most professional sometimes you have to drop people – not everyone is cut out to be a lifeguard.'

'I don't like doing that and I feel sad for the person. I wouldn't want that happening to me, but I have to look at the whole team. It might fall apart in five years because I made the wrong choices. I need to look at the bigger picture. It's not just about the individuals.'

Hoppo draws on the tough exterior that his country-bred Dad had to get him through at times.

'It can take its toll when you have to make decisions like letting people go or pulling people up for things they are doing. I can often get the flack, when people disagree with what I'm saying when I'm having a go at them. That builds up in me. It probably comes from my dad – he didn't let anyone see his emotions or his vulnerable side either. I probably don't take enough down time.'

'But at the same time I have changed from that. I realize that it's not the only way to go. I think there's another way to go. Sure at certain times that's the right thing but I don't think all the time. Say for example with the guys – I don't give out a lot of compliments. Some people criticise me for that, but I think it's a part of the job that they should be doing anyway – so get on with it! When you do something outstanding or exceptional then yes, I will let you know. And when I give a compliment they sit up and notice, and when I get angry about something they notice that too!'

'After a big day – we all get together if we can and have a few beers and relax and chat and talk about different things – just change the topics and relax and put things into perspective. We give each other a bit of a bagging and make it light hearted.'

'I do a lot of ski paddling or I go and play golf on my days off to get away from the beach. I try not to get to the beach too much on my days off. You sort of get sick of the beach sometimes! That's not to say that if there's a nice wave I'll go down and catch it!'

KERRBOX

Kerrbox reckons he is the rat out of the bunch, which is an odd expression for him to use because he hates rats with a passion.

'Trouble always seems to find me,' he says. 'I'm always in trouble, and Harries calls me Elvis, as I'm the king and I also have nine lives. I've partied with some of the coolest stars, like Johnny Rotten, even Robert de Niro and Public Enemy, Chris Joannou from Silverchair. We've all been surfing and hanging out.'

Some of the guys even date the same girls. 'I started dating one of Reidy's old girlfriends and I ended up getting engaged to her briefly', says Kerboxx. 'I bought her an expensive ring and she tossed it back at me, I'm still trying to find the right woman to settle down and have a family with. But I seem to have had some of the worst relationships in the history of dating! I've been through about four longterm relationships. I seem to pick the wrong girls. I like them young, unlike Maxi who likes them older. When Maxi and Hoppo travelled to Europe, they met up with two women, a mother and daughter and went out with them. Maxi ended up with the mother and Hoppo went out with the daughter!'

'These guys that I work with here are in some ways like my family – we know each other really well and we've been through good times and bad times. We've seen each other at our best and worst that's for sure.'

CHAPTER 10

A lifeguard's duty: not just sun and surf

You can be talking and joking and suddenly someone is in serious trouble and they need you. Now. The Bondi Lifeguards are what is called a 'first response' emergency team. After an incident, their job is to help the person to the next stage and hand them on – into the back of an ambulance, into the police station, into a hospital or returned back to family or friends.

They always go beyond what many think is realistic to save someone, to bring them back from near death. Most of the time they win. Not least because of the latest equipment they have on the beach ready and primed at all times. Not an easy task when there are sometimes 40,000 people on the beach.

Death is a daily possibility for Bondi Beach Rescue, but it came as a shock to all of them when each experienced it first hand.

The north headland of Bondi, Ben Buckler, has sandstone cliffs that drop dramatically down to the sea. Before they get to the bottom there is a massive flat rock platform, projecting out wide into the raging Pacific Ocean. At low tide and when the surf is calm, fisherman use it to reel in their catch. Young teenagers jump from the end of the rocks into the sea and swim to the beach. And rock climbers use the cliff to test their rope skills and strength against the sheer cliff.

But there's a sad and tragic side to Ben Buckler. Suicide rates among teenagers are increasing. As Bondi is home to a large teenage and transient population, it gets its share of misfortune. One of the increasing tasks of Bondi Lifeguard is to pick up the pieces in the aftermath of such a tragic decision.

The lifeguards also need to deal with the police, who have to investigate every suicide – have they been thrown off or have they jumped themselves? How did the person die? Was it a head injury or drowning? The lifeguards have to report clearly on the situation as they found it, what they did and when, and what the conditions were like at the time. Every lifeguard deals with death and tragedy in a different way. But they all have access to professional help and assistance to get them through trauma and back to work.

Hoppo says that dealing with death is something that you get used to, and it affects how you deal with death in your personal life as well.

'You accept death when you don't know and love the person yourself. But for me, my father is chronically ill now. He signed a do not resuscitate form. So does that mean I will have to watch him die, against all my training, because I won't be able to resuscitate him? But having dealt with a lot of situations and deaths over the years, it also helps you in your personal life.'

MAXI: 'IF I COULD STOP 100 SUICIDES, THAT WOULD BE GOOD!'

Since he joined the lifeguards, Maxi has experienced a lot of major emergency situations where there is the threat of death or actual death while working in America.

'When I had been working here for a while I applied to do some work in the USA to see what happens over there. I was 18 when I applied to the Deaths and Fire Control Department – they work with the lifeguards in the USA. I thought I would go in the winter when there wasn't much happening here in Bondi. I got a position in Florida, in a place called Destin and had experience in lifeguard firefighting. I attended to a lady who had shot herself and

I also went to a plane crash in the ocean. Then I did an intensive care ride along with the paramedics – involving a girl who had gone head on into a car. That was pretty full on but it gave me some good experience and I just had to deal with it. So you could say I have seen a fair bit of death but I have also seen people come to life.'

'Doing this sort of work you have to have a good relationship with the local police and the paramedics team. We're calling on them a lot! The Bondi Police Station is only just round the corner so they always come quickly.'

'Once we had a pack of thieves on the beach stealing stuff from everybody, and it was getting really ugly. When we hit them up they got really out of control, it was a big gang and they were armed with knives. The police came down and they had about 20 policeman in uniforms and cars and undercovers. So in a situation like that we're really relying on the police to get it all under control as there is only so much that we can do.'

'We're allowed to do a citizen's arrest and we can keep them under control and hold them until the police come. In other words, if someone is punching my head in I can punch them back, but I can't throw the first punch.'

'I've done a few of these arrests. And I've had two run off on me! But I'm a good runner and by the time I catch up with them they are pretty puffed out! I've chased a guy all the way from Bronte Beach to Charing Cross! That's about 4k!'

'There's so many people here at Bondi all year and of course we have a lot of kids too. So yeah we get tied up sometimes in big family arguments where we have to call the police, and there are custody issues as well, and people get really mad and we have to calm it down.'

'There's this place north of Bondi that faces the Pacific Ocean called The Gap, which is a huge drop down into the ocean onto rock platforms. It's famous for being a place where people commit suicide and there are all these signs there trying to stop people from doing it, and to call for help. A lot of kids jump off the cliffs too. I have experienced this and have developed an understanding of the aftermath of suicide and the impact it has on the kid's families. We have to go out to the headland and retrieve the kids once they jump. The police won't go in the water.'

'On my first day in Bronte Beach I went to a guy who jumped off a cliff. Now I have done about 7 suicides – the youngest was about 16 years of age and was in a bad way. That really affected me. All the ones I have attended to have been really bad. I don't know if you can have a good one actually, so they all are pretty horrific. One guy had really bad head trauma when he jumped off the cliff.'

'The kids are so young and the ones I have seen have really affected me, and I started to think if there was anything we could do to stop it happening. If I could only just stop one or two kids from jumping that would be something. If I could stop 100 well that would be good too of course! So I got involved in a charity for kids called Headspace and it's been really great for me to feel that I'm giving something back.'

REIDY: 'YOU CAN'T TAKE TOO MUCH TO HEART.'

'The influx of tourists here is just incredible. Most Australians do know how to swim and how to stay safe on the beach, plus they live here and generally just go home at the end of the day. But we're also dealing with people visiting from all over Australia and all over the world. And some people just don't make it home.'

'We do a lot of body retrieval work. We have go out on the jet skis and pick up any bodies that haven't been able to be rescued. It's not just suicides, but also people who have fallen in the ocean and drowned and are brought by the currents to Bondi, Bronte or Tamarama.'

'The problem is that we can't leave the tower unmanned, and you can't leave someone on the beach on their own. So sometimes it gets tricky, but that's when we really appreciate the trainees, because they can fill some gaps when we have to go out and do stuff.'

'The suicide work is stressful there's no doubt about that. For me that really hit home when I was having a relationship with this girl who had depression issues and at the same time I had to deal with a suicide at work.'

'One day I pulled a 30 year old woman off the rocks and had to get her into the body bag. The helicopter came out to try and winch it off but there was a fierce southerly wind blowing and the winch on the helicopter wouldn't do it so I went and got her. For about the next six months of my life I had this terrible situation when my friend kept calling me to say she was going to kill herself, and I would find her at The Gap just around the corner from where I had to get this girl.'

'One of the first days of the season last year in Bronte a guy jumped off the headland. The boys did an amazing job getting him back breathing even though he had broken every bone in his body. The guys rescued him and he was alive for long enough in the hospital at least for his family to say goodbye. How do we deal with that? Well we can get as much help as we like professionally in dealing with it. But you know for me I know that the bullying I had at school for being an overweight teenager led me to be the person I am today. You can't take too much to heart, I don't take it too personally. I reckon we're really lucky in this country. In other parts of the world there are dead people in the middle of the street, and no one is picking them up. We're protected from that.'

'A lot of people contact me on social media because of the work I do and because they see us on the TV dealing with all sorts of traumatic situation. Like a girl who had to deal with her first CPR incident, and she messaged me saying it's been a year since she was involved and she was still thinking about it. I said she had to say to herself that you did the best job that you could at the time and move on from that. Rely on yourself that you did the best that you could.'

'I'm lucky as well that we have such a great team and we support each other when there's trauma to deal with. I think kids today get babied a lot – you know there is a point where you need to have self-discipline and get through things. Yeah I use my background to get me through the tough times, because I know I have survived. I've come through it.'

HARRIES: 'YOU KNOW THAT THERE'S ALWAYS GOING TO BE PAIN AND SUFFERING.'

For a guy with a reputation of being totally interested in his own body image, Harries is surprisingly deep in his philosophy about life and death. And he has used this to deal with many situations of death and suicide.

'I'm not frightened about picking people up in all sorts of incidents. People handle things differently – some people handle death differently. You have paramedics on one side and then people who faint at the sight of it. I guess that is a test of being a lifeguard, you have to be able to handle death and assess the situation and make sure you do the right thing.'

'Once I had a lady trying to commit suicide about 50m away from me. She was in my side vision so I didn't realise it was a person on the rocks. I was on a thinner board than we use now and I waved for my brother to come out and help me.'

'When I finally got to her I put her on the board and caught a big wave all the way to the shore, but she was dead by the time I got there to the beach and there was nothing we could do for her. Her head was so badly damaged it was too late.'

'I know that I couldn't have stopped her from jumping– I only caught her from the corner of my eye at the last minute. And even if I had seen her, and shouted out would she have listened to me? Probably not. Could I have resussed her when I got her on the board? No, I didn't have a defibrillator. But I do wonder sometimes whether I could have prevented it. You can't help asking yourself these questions. My wife is so wise – she says when I'm arguing like that I'm only arguing with myself. The actual body situation doesn't really affect me. But it does affect me when I see the pain in the family's eyes when someone passes. I really feel pain for them. I try not to think too much about parents when they are freaking out, I try to focus on the rescue. That's the hardest time. It's one of those things no matter how many times you do it, you never get used to it. You know that there's always going to be pain and suffering from something like that.'

'The best thing I want to do is at least try and get the kids back long enough for their family to say goodbye, and that might be better for their families. They might be able to give them a cuddle before they go you know? It's really important for us to give the family closure; to give them the body so they can grieve properly. Because you can't dig deep enough into a human to find out how deep that love is for their child or their wife.'

KERRBOX: 'LIFEGUARDING IS MORE THAN HELPING PEOPLE OUT OF THE SURF.'

Kerrbox has a wicked laugh and is generally chuckling about something or other. But when it comes to talking about serious incidents he straightens his back and looks at you straight in the eye.

'Lifeguarding is more than helping people out of the surf. At first when I started I got rattled by the huge job you have to do and the risk that people take and how much they rely on us to get them out of trouble.'

'I mean some days in summer you're looking at 40–50,000 people. When I first started I was thinking oh my god how am I going to handle this? What am I going to do if something really serious happens? And I also didn't know if I was doing the right thing at times. It sounds easy and it looks easier on the television than it really is. You're thinking fast all the time, and you're trying to avoid a situation where someone will die. Once I figured out how to focus on a few things, and not let everything else distract me it got better. I learnt what to look for.'

'If you're confident with yourself that you're watching the most important parts on the beach you can get through but that takes a while to learn. It takes a while to get that through your head. The heart attacks and stuff are there all the time. But we get really good training, excellent training in fact. We train with paramedics and we're always trying to better ourselves with our medical training.'

'You can never plan or know how you're going to feel when you deal with the suicides. You know when we're retrieving the bodies you never know how you're going to react to that. I remember my first one – I couldn't see for three weeks after that. We pulled him out and he was a young kid and I looked straight into his eyes. I tell the young guys now not to look at their faces. Don't look at them – because you never get rid of the image. I could draw a picture of that guy's face now and that was 20 years ago.'

'Every day you wonder what is going to happen at work today? We have gang fights, a lot of stealing, drug overdoses, this year the car launch, a bomb off in the toilets, fires. You name it down here we get it. You never know what you're going to get from one day to another. That's why it's exciting and I wouldn't change it for the world.'

HOPPO: 'A LOT OF THE LIFEGUARDS CAN'T DEAL WITH IT.'

All the Bondi Lifeguard boys have to deal with suicides. Being the boss of the team doesn't mean Hoppo is remote from death and trauma. In fact it's the opposite. He is on the case and on the job every day.

'I remember my first dead body' he says. 'You never forget the face of the person. I had a girl commit suicide off the rocks and when I went to pick her up her head was so badly damaged,' says Hoppo. 'That was bad. I remember I told a guy who was bagging us out a lot about our job. He kept coming down to the tower on his bike and saying well you guys don't work much really do you. Then I told him about that situation I had just dealt with and he changed his mind after that! He realized what we have to do.'

'For anything major like that we get counsellors in for the lifeguards. They will talk to everyone and pick up on different things that we say. They are the experts in seeing if any of us have a problem with it.'

'Mentally you can deal with something at the time – and then you don't realize that something can trigger a recall of that incident later in your life and then you can have major problems and issues. Even if it's six months ago or years ago, it might come back at you if you haven't dealt with it properly and openly at the time.'

'It's the same when people get abused as kids for example, they will suddenly have a breakdown as adults – it's an underlining problem from years ago. There might be a trigger that sets off a lot of deeper stuff. So we're aware of that, and offer that now automatically. It used to be an option but now if we have had to deal with something particularly bad we all just go.'

'Basically we could get a suicide a week – and a lot of them are still alive when we get to them and they don't die straight away. Many are in a really bad place and we have to watch them die often. A lot of the lifeguards have left because they can't deal with it anymore.'

'Me? Yeah I will have some counseling sometimes if I'm involved in a case. They will always say if they need another session – its open and anonymous – you don't have to tell anyone if you're having counseling. It's the same with any emergency first response field of work and we're in that category.'

Hoppo often talks about one incident where they managed to bring back a young man from the dead. He's proud of it as it was filmed at the time from start to finish. And that film is now used as a training video for other Lifeguards.

'We were doing a photoshoot for a magazine down at the water's edge at Bondi. We were running in and out of the water, as a team and then individually, and laughing and joking on the sand. Then we heard somebody calling out that there was someone in the water who needed help.'

'We stopped immediately and ran over to where the commotion was. A young Swedish tourist had pulled a young man out of the water and was calling for help. She had seen him just floating face down.'

'It was a young Japanese man. We pulled him out of the water up to the sand. He was dead. His face was lifeless and there was no pulse and no breathing. So we commenced CPR and someone ran up to the tower to get the defibrilator. We gave him three shocks in five minutes and inbetween we kept working on his chest. The parademics arrived but by the third shock we knew that was pretty much his last chance. Suddenly he started breathing and his pulse came back really strong.'

'We turned him on his side and he threw up all the water he had inside of him. The buzz around a resuscitation is amazing. By the time the ambulance took him away, he was actually talking to us and telling us his name. Later we found out that he had a heart defect that he didn't know about and he had a heart attack while he was swimming with his language teacher and a fellow student.'

'An hour before that he had been up at The Gap walking. If he had had the heart attack up there he wouldn't have survived. By the time the paramedics would have reached him it would have been too late. But because we're right there on the beach, with emergency training and equipment, he made it through. It was one of the most controlled episodes of resuss we have done too – everyone knew their role, and it went really well.'

CHAPTER 11:

There could be a TV show in this you know?

It's the perfect mix for a reality show – dramatic medical emergencies, stunning views of the Pacific Ocean breakers, even more stunning girls in bikinis, good looking guys, an incredible bond and camaraderie among mates. You can't get better than that! It all makes for dynamic watching on TV, and awards too – five Logies (the Australian television industry awards) in fact.

Hoppo describes how it all started in his usual laid-back way.

'Ben Davies worked in TV, writing scripts for Getaway and other shows. Like many of the lifeguards, he went to Waverley College, and he was an experienced surfer and waterman, so in the summer of 2005–2006 he took a part-time job in the lifeguards to supplement his writer's income. What Ben saw every day in the tower and on the beach blew his mind. He had believed that the job was just an easy way to hang out at the beach all day, and never realized what the team was up against. He started talking to Channel Ten, and they finally agreed to do a one-hour special in 2005. They had already made a one-hour emergency special on bush fire fighters, and so they thought a lifeguard one would fit with that.'

Bondi Rescue the TV show was shot with the 'fly on the wall' technique, and aired in 2007. It took off, and a series was commissioned. There are 12 people on the beach when the show is filming – a water camera operator, two land camera operators, two sound engineers, two field producers, two production assistants, a tower director, Ben Davies, who is still involved in the show, and a driver. They are there from 9am till 7pm every day in the summer season – from mid-December through till March.

The show is now approaching its tenth series, something which Hoppo and the boys are really proud of. It has also attracted a huge international following and is distributed worldwide, including in the US, the UK, Sweden, Norway, Germany, Denmark and now throughout Asia. Shows often have over a million viewers in Australia, a consistent record they have been keeping up since the show first started. Nobody thought it would be that popular, and the guys in the tower never thought that what they do everyday would be that fascinating to people not just in Australia, but all over the world. But all you have to do is spend a few hours with the guys in the tower and you're hooked. What's going to happen next? How are they going to get that guy out of the water? Why did that woman collapse?

All the boys on the show have fans all over the world who love to follow their daily lives. They are great guys with a real passion for their job and a genuine 'do your best' commitment to public service.

The TV show has brought with it the spotlight – which for many of the guys has opened up new possibilities in their lives that they could never have thought of. Business ideas, media training, talks to people, charity events and many more opportunities have come along in the TV show beach bag. From that first pilot, the boys hurtled into their celebrity destiny.

MAXI: 'I'M STILL PINCHING MYSELF.'

'What's it like being a celebrity? I still have to pinch myself that I'm on television! I forget half the time! I mean who would have believed that I would be 2013 Cleo Bachelor of the Year!'

Cleo Magazine was Australia's first glossy magazine to run a double spread picture of naked men, just like Playboy was doing. Most of Australia's stars have been the Bachelor of the Year – which they can win without the centrefold!

'Now I have a girlfriend so I'm not a bachelor anymore,' Maxi says quickly! 'Guess what? She needs to learn how to swim! She's a country girl who moved to Sydney and she needs swimming lessons. Lots of people think that's funny but it's the reality for heaps of country kids.'

'I've never had any negative feedback from anyone recognizing me after being on the show. People call out to me and I always say hi. I mean you don't hide when you're at work here do you? You're out and about on the beach all the time. You do get the odd dick head who wants to have a go and stir you up. I just say, "G'day mate!" And then I say "Come on mate don't be like that, I love you!" It kills them when you're nice to them! It's always so funny that.'

'I used to hate learning when I was a kid. Now I understand that you can learn to become successful. I've got a business now called Bad Max, which stands for Beating Anxiety and Depression. I designed and made some T shirts and hoodies with quotes on them about inspiration and being positive. I designed it all myself. I wouldn't mind studying a bit more about running a business. I've also started a business with fellow life guard Jesse Pollock called Ocean Men, doing water safety, surfing lessons, motivational and safety talks, day trips and jet ski rides.'

'I mean it's done pretty well but I don't know if some people felt sorry for me and that's why they bought it! I'm not sure if I would have done that if it hadn't been for the show and all the positive people I have met. I'm taking a bit of a break from it now and seeing what's next. I'm thinking of expanding it and so I want to learn how to do that.'

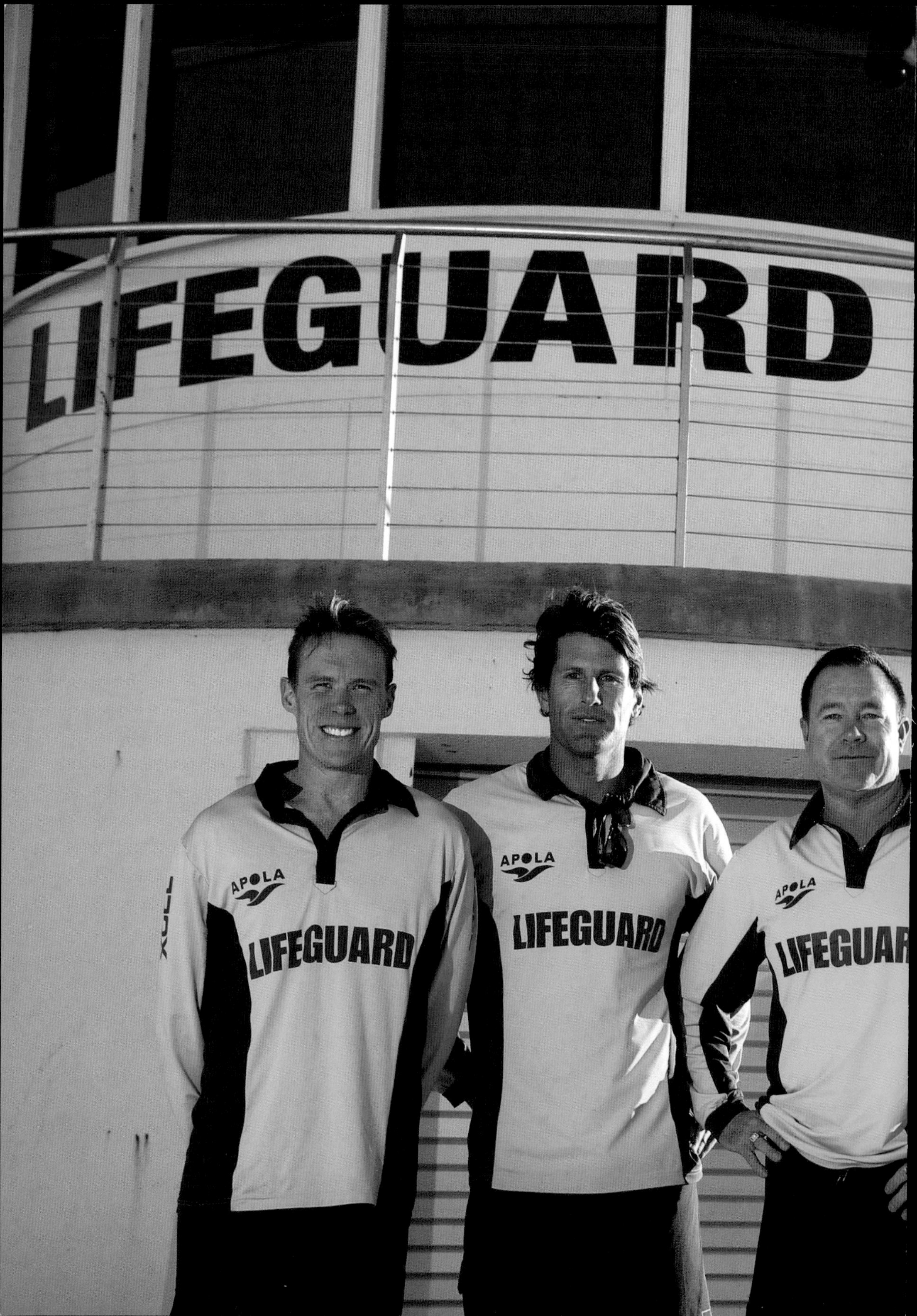
LIFEGUARD
APOLA
LIFEGUARD
APOLA
LIFEGUARD
APOLA

'Being on the show means you get heaps of fans on Facebook and followers on Twitter which is great fun. I don't put up any controversial stuff online. I'm really aware of social media now and what can go around. I'm aware of my image and so I'm happy to be a positive person. I want to inspire young people around the world because they need positivity. I like being on the show because it's fun, but it gives me a chance to try and help young people become what they want to in their life. I wouldn't have been able to raise half as much money for Headspace if it wasn't for the TV show.'

'Me and fellow lifeguard Jesse Pollock rode jet skis from Sydney to Cairns, a total of 3,100km and it took us 16 days. We called it Ride East Coast. Every afternoon we stopped at a Headspace Centre – a youth mental health association that provides support for 13–25 year olds. It mentors them and offers workshops and counseling for depression and suicide. That's the biggest killer for young Australians. We did the ride for them and for people struggling and made a documentary about it as well. We went into the centres and talked to the kids – people who are gay, have anger problems, relationship problems, family problems, are being bullied – all these situations for young people without support can potentially lead to suicides.'

'The kids were interested in us as we deal with a lot of suicides here at Bondi. There are big rock platforms here and a lot of kids jump off the cliffs. I have developed an understanding of the aftermath of suicide and the impact it has on the kids families. It inspired me to try and stop it happening. Stay happy and stay positive was my advice. Everyone is in different situations. And the people round them should realize – you don't want to have someone's suicide on your conscious. That's the message I have for the bullies.'

'I think life is like the weather. You can be the happiest person in the world having a picnic and then there is a storm coming through and then you rush home and have a hot shower and feel better. Then the next day its sunny and everything is okay. My life motto is "It's just a bad day and not a bad life".'

'Going to all these coastal towns I asked people – have you lived here all your life? And they would say yes. What do you mean? I said well if you go 300k in either way you're out of your bubble and you will find yourself. There are so many people who are exactly like you. That person is out there. They don't know how to escape. I mean chicks getting pregnant too early that can lead to mental health issues and suicide. But if they just go out and travel and see a bit of the world just outside them they will see they are just like everyone else.'

'Keep happy and positive is what I want to share with young people out there! Follow me on LifeguardMaxi. To all our overseas fans I want to say we appreciate your support! Without you guys we wouldn't be going into 10 years of being on television!'

REIDY: 'SWIMMING ONE MINUTE, UNCONSCIOUS THE NEXT.'

'I love the TV show and all it does for us at Bondi. Particularly because the show has raised awareness of what lifeguards do and also how they put their lives on the line when they go out saving people.'

'It was the first time that anyone had filmed lifeguards and the daily reality we work with, which is that someone can be swimming one minute and unconscious the next. But at Bondi, the safest end of the beach is the northern end, which is the one farthest away from the street access. So the first part of the beach that anyone comes to when they walk down the road is actually the most dangerous part – the southern end. That's where the strongest rips and rocks are. The show has helped people realize all over the world about the flags and what happens when you go swimming in an area where you're not being looked after. So now we mostly do about 100 rescues in a season whereas we used to do a lot more.'

The show is also a massive burst of publicity for the guys – and brings with it certain 'fringe benefits' in the shape of great looking chicks.

Harries reckons that the Bondi Rescue show has been the greatest thing to happen to lifeguarding. And he's not knocking back the media exposure on TV or radio either.

'It's put us on the map. No one knew what we did. Everyone thought these blokes were a bunch of chick-pulling magnets who tan up and then go and booze up afterwards. But they can see on the TV that the boys work really hard under a lot of pressure. The credibility to have that internationally was amazing. Worth more than gold.'

'People have put this job down in the past you know and it means a lot now that they can see what we actually do on a daily basis – people haven't been able to picture it but now they can. It's not just in a Bondi bubble. One person asked me once how do you measure what you do each day? But we can't measure how many times we are looking through the crowd and detecting problems every day! Well we have 40,000 people sometimes here. It's a massive ask. They all come crying to us when they need us!'

'I remember when the show first started, and I was thinking "this isn't going to be easy!" A lot of us were naughty boys and on the weekends we were up to no good! Just like any other bunch of young blokes! When Kerrbox and I were working on the first pilot, a guy knocked on the door and said look I have just seen a massive shark out at the point there. I said oh yeah? Well it's a seal probably. We get a lot of seals around here. With my luck it may be a mermaid! Or it might have been a dolphin. He said, "Look mate, I have been around here a long time, and I surf and I fish, and this one is massive".

'Then people started ringing into the tower. The guys on the cameras got really excited – wow they were going to get a shark in the first show! So I went out on the jet ski and couldn't see

anything for half and hour. All I could see were about 100 people on the headland screaming at me and pointing at the ocean. They could see it doing a big arc around me in the ocean. Basically it was like an A380 plane coming into Sydney Airport. Then I saw the fin come up – it was around 18-foot and it was a Great White – they got a shot of it and the shot went international.'

'Then we got the show two days later! Surprise surprise! All the guys are always kidding me that I don't want to put my head in the water and ruin my hair style for the TV cameras! Anyway, after the show went to air Alan Jones rang me while I was in the gym and I hate my training being interrupted. He asked me 'So Mr Carroll what did you really see out there? "Well" I said, "mark my words Mr Jones. We have a predator amongst us!"

'We are well known personalities at Bondi now, we are recognised by the public on a daily basis. A few times I have been mistaken for Harry Nightingale was when I was in the running for Cleo Bachelor of the Year, alongside Maxi! Maxi got it, and I'm so glad for him because I'm not a bachelor any more! But at the time I got a call from the publicist about a story calling me Harry Nightingale – and I said you've got the wrong Harry! He would have gone home to his wife and said, "Hey I'm in the running for Cleo Bachelor of the Year!" That was a bit of fun!'

'The nice thing about being a famous lifeguard is that we get involved in some incredible life stories. Like the other week, there was a lady from Bulgaria who was partially blind aged 65. She had fallen off the platform and onto the train line at Central Station and a train ran over her and severed her legs. Her dream was to come down and meet the lifeguards and have a ride on the jet ski. And so she did and it was beautiful to meet with her. I love to help people in that way. And I have also been involved in the Royal Children's Hospital raising money for the kids. I did a 64k walk with Libby Tricket and Daniel Geil for Westmead Children's Hospital to raise money for them.'

'We are always helping people. You know what I think of these guys here that I work with?

These lifeguards? Are they TV celebrities? My word they are. Are they heroes? Yes they save lives. Would they give you the shirt off their back? Damn straight they would. They are rich in character and rich in love. All of them. And that's why people want to watch them on the TV.'

KERRBOX: 'THEY NEVER GET IN OUR WAY'

Kerrbox thought that the TV show was really scary at first. After all the changes they had to bring in and the complete revitalization of the service, they weren't sure if the film would make them look bad.

'We didn't know if having a crew following us every day would be a good thing. Are we going to do the wrong thing? Are they going to show us making mistakes? And I swear all the time! I'm always getting bleeped on the TV! I always get in trouble from my mum! In fact it was my mum who said, "Oh my God, I didn't know that's what you did all day!" when she first saw it.'

'We resuscitated a guy on the beach the other day and then I went home and pretended nothing had happened. You try not to take your job home with you. And my mum saw that episode and was really a bit shocked. So if that was my Mum saying that then I guess that's what everyone around the world thinks! It works so well because we have a great understanding and relationship with the film crew. We trust them, as there could be some embarassing things we don't want on, but we know they are trying to make a show. Sometimes we ask them to leave us alone. And sometimes I say, "Get out of my face!" or "Look drop the camera and help me out here!"'

'I had a really bad spinal injury case a few years back and I needed the crewmen's help. They dropped their cameras on the spot. One of the water camera guys was holding up some people a few years ago and they were drowning him. He had to crack his camera over a guy's head because he was going to drown him until we got there. But they never get in our way. Sometimes we might slow down a bit to let them catch up, or we give them a heads up, but we don't ever change for them. I've been to three of the guy's weddings so I've become really good friends with them.'

All of the boys do some charity work because of their identities on the TV. Their participation can really make a difference to raising profile and funds. Kerrbox has been working with the Schizophrenia Association on a fundraiser that they call the Stop Swearing for Schizophrenia campaign.

'Yeah it's a joke that I'm on that because of my constant cursing! They came to me and asked me to introduce a swear jar at work as they saw me on the TV and realised I was the perfect fit for them!'

'I do it with Fitzy and Wippa on Nova Radio as well. I think I swore in my first sentence when I started on the show! I have been working with them for 5–6 years now, wearing their hats and gear as well. Live to Give is another charity I work with. I'm really happy to do that if it makes a difference from being on the TV.'

'Harries is up for charity work too, and we did the Full Monty together for a charity. Someone approached us and asked us if we would go nude in front of an audience. We hadn't even seen the movie at that time and we said yeah we will do it. We ended up packing out a 900-seater venue in Darling Harbour and raising a heap of money! We were told we couldn't go completely naked by the owner, but sure enough by the time we got to the end, yep we were in the nude.'

'I've done a lot of charity work with my surfing mates as well. In 2010, I joined a celebrity challenge against Australian professional surfers Kelly Slater, Taj Burrow and Mick Fanning at Bondi as part of the Boost Mobile SurfSho. We were just hammered by fans trying to get a look at everyone!'

'We had boxer Danny Green, TV presenters Jason Dundas and Mike Whitney, and Bondi Vet Dr Chris Brown to compete for a $5,000 donation to charity. We donated it to The Smile Train, which provides free cleft surgery for children in developing countries. It was fantastic to be part of a big surf event at Bondi.'

KERRBOX: A LESSON LEARNT

Being famous has also taught Kerrbox a lot of things about himself, and things he has had to change. He ended up as Today Tonight headline news in 2013, and it isn't something he was proud of.

'It made me realise that I'm recognised wherever I go now. I'm not just a surfer and a lifeguard – the show has been going on for about 9 years now and people know who I am. I lost a mobile phone on the Gold Coast, and yes, I admit I was hungover. I was trying to get assistance from a girl at the front desk of the hotel I was staying at, and she wasn't helping me – and I ended up swearing at her as I was so frustrated. I went way over the top. I realised it quickly at the time and apologised to her and sent her flowers.'

'Two weeks later I got a call from Channel Ten. They said we need you to write an apology to the hotel you were in a few weeks ago. I explained I'd already apologised and it was accepted and it was all done and dusted, but they said I was headline news. "Reality TV star loses it on the Gold Coast" was one headline and "Celebrity Meltdown' was another."'

'Someone had stood behind me with a mobile phone and videoed me. That was a big lesson for me – I don't mind talking about it, I was really embarrassed and hid under the bed for about two weeks at home. So to try and balance it out, I did the Nickleodeon Slime Fest when celebrities get slimed. It's changed my life heavily that incident. I'm pretty outgoing and I love to have a beer and have a good time, I do attract a certain type of person which is fine – but I have to choose now who I party with. I have had a big reality check of late and I have changed my ways.'

'They found my phone! I have lost 19 phones! Everyone who knew me just said "Oh no, here he goes again", because they know I lose phones all the time but the poor girl didn't deserve to be abused and I know that.'

'It taught me we have to be really careful everywhere we go – airports, restaurants, we get stopped everywhere we go. More so when we are all together. If there is a bunch of us then we are instantly recognised. And that's what my social life is like now.'

'Nowadays, Dean Gladstone is right behind me keeping me fit. I'm lucky to have him in my life looking over my shoulder and keeping me on the straight and narrow. Deano keeps me fit through the winter (which is something that I hate having to do!) – and in return I take him surfing. We love surfing big waves together. I am actually scared of him he is such a big part of my life! Ha ha ha!'

HOPPO: 'WE MAKE IT ALL LOOK SO EASY.'

Hoppo really supported the plan to make the TV show and he could see it was perfect timing for the lifeguarding service.

'I really wanted to have the TV show at Bondi. When Ben started talking about it I thought, yes that's a great idea! I didn't think what we were doing was that interesting for the general public – I just thought we were picking up people on a board and bringing them back to shore, what's so interesting about that? But I wanted to see if we could use it to get some safety messages out there.'

'You know the guys here are so good at doing their job – they make it look so easy. They make it look easy to paddle out the back of the waves and grab someone – I can tell you it's not that easy! We've had football teams down here to do training sessions with us and they are fit as anything. We put them on the rescue boards and they can't kneel and they fall off and they can't hold their breath under waves.'

'My main concern was getting the show through the Council regulations. They were okay about it as long as the proper procedures were followed. So the production company put together a pilot – I was a bit conservative about it originally because I didn't want it to expose us and I didn't want it to portray us in a negative light. We had good equipment and great guys. Then it twigged with me that one thing we lacked was profile. Nobody knew that since 1913 there have been professional lifeguards here. We're not as visible to the public.'

'Back then around 2006 there were only three of us on the beach, coping with 30,000 crowds, so we blended in. We needed a profile and I wanted to show people what professional lifeguards actually do. And at the same time we could be giving out a surf safety message so I thought yes, that might be okay. The cameras came in and started filming. Up until then, normally the cameras on TV shows captured people as they came into hospital or being interviewed after an ordeal. In this case filming started right from the point of an emergency situation developing, right from the beginning. It was unique. The film crew had to learn how to capture it – sometimes there are so many things happening the show could just look like mad confusion. So they had to learn how to follow up certain stories and stick with that. We didn't predict the show would be so successful – or realize that it would also become about us – we thought it would just be about the rescues.'
'But the guys who work in the service are amazing guys – they have this sort of larrikin

quality to them I guess, but then they are completely serious and really dedicated to their work. They will go over and above the line to make sure they do their best. And that makes them stand out. It's also successful because it's about why we do it – we want people to know what lifeguards do, we want to put out the surf safety message, and we want to rescue people and save people's lives. So that is our Why. We never knew that this fitted in with a business model theory! This sounds like a TED talk theory lesson! I guess the show had a precedent with Baywatch in LA, but our show was real, and so were our lifeguards.'

'When all the footage went back to the executives they said hang on a minute – this is an episode and a half – plus an hour special. Then there was enough first aid episodes and people with big gashes in their heads to make a six part series. Then after the first year it was an eight-part series – then they did 13 episodes from then on.'

'This beach brings heaps of celebrities to it – Rowan Atkinson (Mr Bean), actor Zac Effron, and, of course, Richard Branson – I could go on and on. I'd probably have to say Indian cricketer Sachin Tendulkar was the most exciting person to meet because I've always been a huge cricket fan. I played a bit when I was at school and in my teenage years, and have watched him over the years and it's amazing to shake hands with someone of his status.' 'We mix with quite a few actors now – a lot of people come up to me and say hey you're the same now you're on TV, but I'm just playing myself! In the cast list we are all listed as 'himself'.'

Hoppo has had plenty of offers to work as a model or an extra on film after his appearances on Bondi Rescue. He's done some modeling and catwalk appearances and has doubled for actors in action television series such as *Water Rats* and *Police Rescue*. He also appeared in the award-winning movie *Muriel's Wedding*. He says he prefers live TV, though, it's much faster and there is more action – rather than standing around waiting for the next scene.

'They don't do any takes on our show – if they miss it they miss it. There's no going back. It happens like that because they film it with up to 24 cameras, most of which are tiny 'go-pro' cameras attached to bikes, jetskis, and surfboards. Microphones are attached to the lifeguard's armbands to make sure they capture all the dialogue in the water, and as well they have two manned crews following the lifeguards on the beach. Most of the TV team have been the same camera and sound guys and producers – which means they are part of the team now. They are spotting potential situations now too – we could put them on as internships!'

'It's an unbreakable rule that filming never interferes or takes priority over rescues. In fact when you're in the moment in an adrenelin rush you forget about the cameras. You could be talking about anything in the rhino ATV – in fact they put together a bloopers tape every year and it's really funny. The first year there was a lot of trial and error about what would work on the show. In the first year they just recorded everything. I asked one girl who was recording everything how it was going, and she said it had been very educational! I said, "Well yes, I can imagine what you've been listening to!"'

'Now we have won Logie Awards over the past six years for the show. Our first Logie was really surreal – standing up there as lifeguards in front of a room full of actors and presenters and here were a couple of beach bums winning an award! We won it for the Most Popular Factual Program five times.'

'Yes you could say that my life has changed a lot since the show – hey everyone likes getting attention no matter who you are! People all round the world like to have photos taken with me – from London to Dubai. We're putting a smile on people's faces – and if you're putting yourself out there in the public then you need to give something back. Young kids and young people look up to you and respect you, so you've got to keep smiling and talking to people because they are our fans! And we wouldn't be where we are without them!'

CHAPTER 12:

Rescues: never a dull moment, always changing.

Rescuing people from the Pacific Ocean is not like swimming 50m in a pool and getting out again. Every individual who gets into trouble has a different way of reacting to their situation. Plus, the conditions of the ocean, the strength of the current, the temperature and their level of fitness comes into play massively when the lifeguards are trying to bring them into shore. The rips can be running strong or not at all, and Reidy reckons that the days when the beach is flat is when they get the most rescues. People just don't see the dangers of the ocean.

There are various manuals, rescue instructions and procedures that are available, but sometimes the lifeguards just have to go on their gut instinct to work out which is the best way to get the rescued person to the ambulance the fastest.

Being a good lifeguard is not something you can learn overnight and most of the lifeguards bring to the job years they have clocked up already reading the ocean through surfing. Being a professional ocean lifeguard means you have to be outstanding at board work and surfing. You've also got to be good at communication – clear in your signals and clear in your instructions. You also have to be highly motivated and fast – and constantly aware and vigilant, so that you can stop accidents before they happen.

The APOL (Australian Association Professional Ocean Lifeguards) lists the qualities that lifeguards need to possess – they have to be physically fit, highly skilled in swimming, able to use first aid equipment, capable of remaining constantly alert, able to read the changing ocean and weather conditions, identifying hazards and risks, and acting fast and efficiently to use their knowledge, skill and determination to preserve or save human life. The ability to be constantly alert is a skill that not everybody has. It's why most of the Bondi Lifeguards can't sit still for long.

All of the lifeguards have stories to tell about one incident that sticks in their mind, or one situation where they knew it was touch and go. It's why they need to be so fit, and why they all need to work together to make sure they have as many successful outcomes as possible.

REIDY: 'WE'VE GOT A PULSE, WE'VE GOT A PULSE!'

No other place does New Year's Eve or Christmas like Bondi. Christmas is a big day on Bondi Beach with thousands of people wanting to be photographed having Christmas in the sun..

'Christmas is our busiest period!' says Reidy. 'And it's more complicated because people have had too much to drink either that day or the day before. I guess the most frustrating thing for me is the stupid things the public do. The worst thing for us is people not watching their kids. You know sometimes its really hard waiting with a distressed kid when their parents have failed to realise they are missing.'

'Christmas time is also a season when most of the English and Irish come to the beach and they generally don't wear sunscreen. So they are leaving the beach as red as a beetroot and you know that they will not be able to sleep for a week. Admittedly you can't help also seeing the funny side of that – you can't take everything really seriously.'

'At Christmas time we are on the megaphone all day, especially if it's sunny weather. I know that at the end of the day you can't get too annoyed with people because they don't know about swimming. Lots of people from India and Asia just haven't learned how to swim. Then you have inexperienced surfboard riders drifting into the flags or people swimming outside the flags – you can't get too stressed about that. You just have to keep reminding people. You can't scream and you can't get aggressive. Some lifeguards take everything to heart – but you can't do that at Bondi.'

'Some people will leave their kids to play in the water and then go and lie down on the beach facing away from the surf! They are not even watching them. Kids can easily get caught up in a dangerous rip. We are often walking around the beach trying to find parents as we have rescued kids out of the water and they are pretty distressed. Then we can't find their parents. I have been in so many situations where I have a kid on a board and I am calling out for their parents and can't find them. That really annoys me. I can't understand it.'

'It's just that people can drown really quietly. They don't always make much noise – some of them do but a lot don't. I'll never forget in 2012, when a young student named Ryan Kim had come to Bondi for a swim. The surf was huge, six foot plus. We had the flags up. At Bondi, if you don't have flags up people swim where ever they want, so even when the waves are seriously big we have to find the safest place we can, put flags up and monitor them closely. On this day we also had undercurrents. This happens when a lot of water is pushing in at the same time a lot of water is trying to go out and if you're not a very good swimmer you are going to struggle. Hence the golden rule, RESPECT the ocean!'

'I was standing on the beach waiting to change over on the jet ski. I was waiting for him to come back to shore in front of the tower and pick me up. I had no radio – I was waiting for his. Suddenly one of our ATVs goes screaming past me on the beach. Straight away I thought, okay, something's happened. As I looked down the beach I noticed the jet ski racing back to shore down between the flags, with someone on the back.'

'I started running to where they were about to land. As I got closer I could see them dragging a man off the back of the ski and up the beach. He was purple and floppy - lifeless. Straight away, I knew it was going to take good teamwork and all our training if we were going to bring this guy back.'

'I came in and held his head. We worked on Ryan for about 3 minutes, I could see the guys were doing good compressions on Ryan's chest – they have to be hard enough to be effective and sometimes you can even break ribs, it's basically manually pumping a heart by pushing down on it with brute force. One of the other lifeguards pelted up with the defib machine. When we got the pads of the defib machine on him it checked for a heart rhythm and reported that there wasn't any. Then it instructed us to check for a pulse. I could feel a faint pulse of blood running through his artery, the main one that runs down from your head. That feeling is like no other in the world! He was alive! We had brought him back! "We've got a pulse!" I shouted. A few days later Ryan turned up to surprise us. He told us what happened from his point of view and it really is amazing.'

'He got hit by about three waves in a row. He couldn't get any air. He told us that it was like falling asleep. He said as he was blacking out, everything became quite peaceful. He could see these films of his life going by and it was so quiet. He saw his family and friends and he said he could "feel time". He said it was just all black and quiet. Then he remembers hearing a clapping sound and me and Chappo saying "we've got a pulse, we've got a pulse!" And it brought him back.'

HARRIES: 'RIGHT PLACE, RIGHT TIME!'

Harries loves his job at Bondi because every day is different and unexpected. He also loves it because it's meant he can do other things that he is passionate about – competing in Ironman and lifeguard challenges, and now as a Dad, spending time with his little boy and wife Emily. He's a champion board paddler and waterman, and won the 2009 Lifeguard Challenge amongst others, but there was one incident at Bondi that had nothing to do with the water. Harries has never forgotten the car incident, as it was one of the strangest days on the beach. He reckons it was something that just shows how unpredictable a day in the life of a lifeguard is.

'It was a rainy day and not a lot of people were on the beach. Harrison called out on the radio from the tower and said there was a car on the beach! There was no one on the beach but there was one car – right up the south end near Backpackers Rip.'

'Funnily enough I had just been updating our procedures and operations manual for incidents on the beach, and I did have a procedure for a car on the beach. It could be kids who've pinched a car, or a driver who is drunk and has just swerved off from the road. In the manual it says go up to the person and politely inform them that no vehicles are allowed on the beach, and see if you can get them to remove it.'

'So I headed down to the car, with Bacon and Adriel Young, and I was laughing and thinking it was somebody's idea of a joke. But when I got there, there was a 91-year old man sitting in the car draped over the steering wheel. People were just staring at him and he was obviously in distress. I asked him his name, and he said he had a bit of chest pain I thought he could be about to have a heart attack. Actually the pain was from the seat belt and he wasn't having a heart attack. The man was Russian, and he had just blacked out while he was driving, his car kept going, flew off the promenade and landed on the beach.'

'That incident could have been an utter catastrophe at Bondi on a sunny day. People sitting up on the hill on the grass, having a capuccino and watching the surf, would have just been mown down by that car. It could have easily been a very tragic event that would have gone down in the history books with multiple deaths and injuries. We were so lucky it was cloudy and wet.'

'The other rescue that stands out for me is what we call Black Sunday, when we did over 250 rescues in one day. This was in 2005, and it was similar to the one way back in 1938, when they had a lot of deaths caused by a flash rip – when waves just come in close to each other and there's nowhere for the water to go but straight out again.'

'On Black Sunday it was only a 3 foot surf but the rips were taking people off the sandbanks and moving them around. It was a really hot day so the beach was packed – it was high summer in January. '

'Even though the surf was small, there was a weird sandbank shape, a bit like a horseshoe, and if you fell off that you were suddenly in pretty deep water and being dragged out. There was about 40,000 people on the beach, and we kept telling people to get out of the water but it was to control them all.'

'Kerrbox, Reidy and myself were on duty – amongst others. We were so busy, that at one stage I had eight people on the jetski and it was like a submarine under water, just putting along – they were all holding on but going under the water. I got them to shore and then there was another person struggling out in the same place. I was screaming into the radio – get that person now! How they all survived is beyond me. People didn't realize how serious it was. The way we were pulling people in we were like ferries filling up with people at Circular Quay!'

'The next day we worked out the stats, and I think we ended up rescuing over 250 people. I had ten people on one board at the same time and we were there for hours and hours. We were completely exhausted by the end of that day.'

'You know since we have become famous lifeguards our lives are about mixing with the media all the time. But all of us, we are always first and foremost lifeguards and our job is to save people's lives. We never stop doing that. One time I was standing up at North Bondi with

Hoppo and we were checking out some modeling photographs that a guy was going to put in a magazine about us. Suddenly I hear crash and bang. What's that? A wheelbarrow? Suddenly a guy screams "Help!" An 85 year old has gone into a bus. Next thing Hoppo and I are dragging him out from under the bus and giving him resuss and trying to get him back. What does it matter about the photos? It means more to me that I can get this guy back for long enough to say goodbye to his family. I ran from the photos and never got to see them again. It meant more to me to be there for that older guy.'

'I think the reason I am on this earth is to help people – it happens to me so many times that I happen to be at the right place in the right time. I've been in situations with people hit by trucks, buses, falling off cliffs, people on lonely stretches of beach where I am the only one and they suddenly need resuss and next minute I'm in the paper. I've also learnt from my mistakes – everyone makes mistakes. You become better from them.'

KERRBOX: 'ONE GNARLY RESCUE'

Kerrbox says that you never know what is going to happen from one day to the next when you work at Bondi. 'You just never know what situation is going to develop, but you just try and prepare yourself.' He admits that some things that the public do really get to him and he gets really annoyed about it. But he also knows it's part of the job to take that and get on with it.

Kerrbox talks about one rescue incident that shows to him the value of a good working team. It also shows how valuable knowledge of the local conditions are when you are working at Bondi. It was a few years ago now but it has never left him. It's a massive statement when Kerrbox says this incident was probably the most difficult rescue he has done in 20 years. It was pouring with rain and a huge surf was running out the back of Bronte. Bronte surf is dangerous at the best of times, but in this case it was about an 8- to 10-foot surf. A Tongan man went out snorkelling in the sea, for a reason that Kerrbox still doesn't understand because in those conditions there's no way you can see anything through a face mask.

'I don't know how he got out there. None of us do. We didn't even know that he was there. He had jumped into the water at the back of the Waverley Cemetery, south of Bronte Beach. You can get down onto the rock platforms there, depending on the tides, and you can get into the water. But it's really dangerous and the swell onto the rocks is really strong. You can easily get smashed badly on those rocks. You have to know what you are doing when you are jumping off rocks. Apart from being cut to pieces, you can get smashed back on the rocks from the current.'

'Someone came running to us in Bronte and told us that someone was in trouble. So I grabbed two tubes and jumped into the ocean with a board to try and get to him. I was battling through the surf – it was huge and the current was going all over the place. I looked around and there's Hoppo right behind me. He hadn't missed a beat, and he was backing me up on another board. When we got to him, we found he was a big guy, he was in a bad way, he had been taking in a lot of water and was losing consciousness.'

'We got him onto one of the boards, and then we swam behind him and took it in turns to just push, push, push, him along towards Tamarama. We had to shove the other board into the shore so we could take it in turns to push him along. It took us about 40 minutes to get him close to the beach. There was no room on the board for us as this guy was so big.'

'But the surf was massive and the current was really strong and was driving us onto the rocks, which it does as it goes around the corner towards Tamarama. It was going to be really difficult to get him into the shore. It's what you call a gnarly rescue!'

'That rescue really brought it home to me how us lifeguards have to really rely on each other in some rescue situations. I think if Hoppo hadn't been there I would probably have either lost the guy, or got into a lot of trouble myself. If it wasn't for us that guy was going to drown. He couldn't swim, and he was semi-unconscious lying on the board.'

'I mean until you are actually out there and experiencing that situation – in the surf with the waves hammering you, trying to push somebody along and keep them afloat, and not go under yourself at the same time – you don't realise how much our experience kicks in. You have someone's life in your hands and so you are trying your best to make the right decisions while you are battling the surf yourself.'

'So we decided we would put the two tubes around him and then at the right time we would push the board away and let the waves just pummel us to the beach. There was no other way we were going to get in. We couldn't go out on the rocks. It was just the three of us tied together with the tubes. We let the surf just push us towards the beach. The surf was too big to take a board, and if a wave had hit him he wouldn't have come up. Because he was so big we wouldn't have been able to hold him up either.'

'We had to get our timing exactly right. We had to push him on the board across the front of the beach and then swing to the shore and make a go for it – the whole time being pummelled by the waves. If we had gone in too quickly then we would have been dragged on to the rip running to the rocks and been taken out again.'

'We had big cuts and scratches from the weight of the guy, and friction burns from the tubes smashing into our skin. It was just one out of many situations where I've relied on Hoppo. I also rely on him in my personal life as well. We know we can get each other through it and then we can carry on.'

Typical for Kerrbox he always likes to make a joke out of a serious situation!

'But I tell you one thing about Hoppo that I do know, even though our timing was perfect on that occasion – he is a terrible dancer. They call him thunderbirds!'

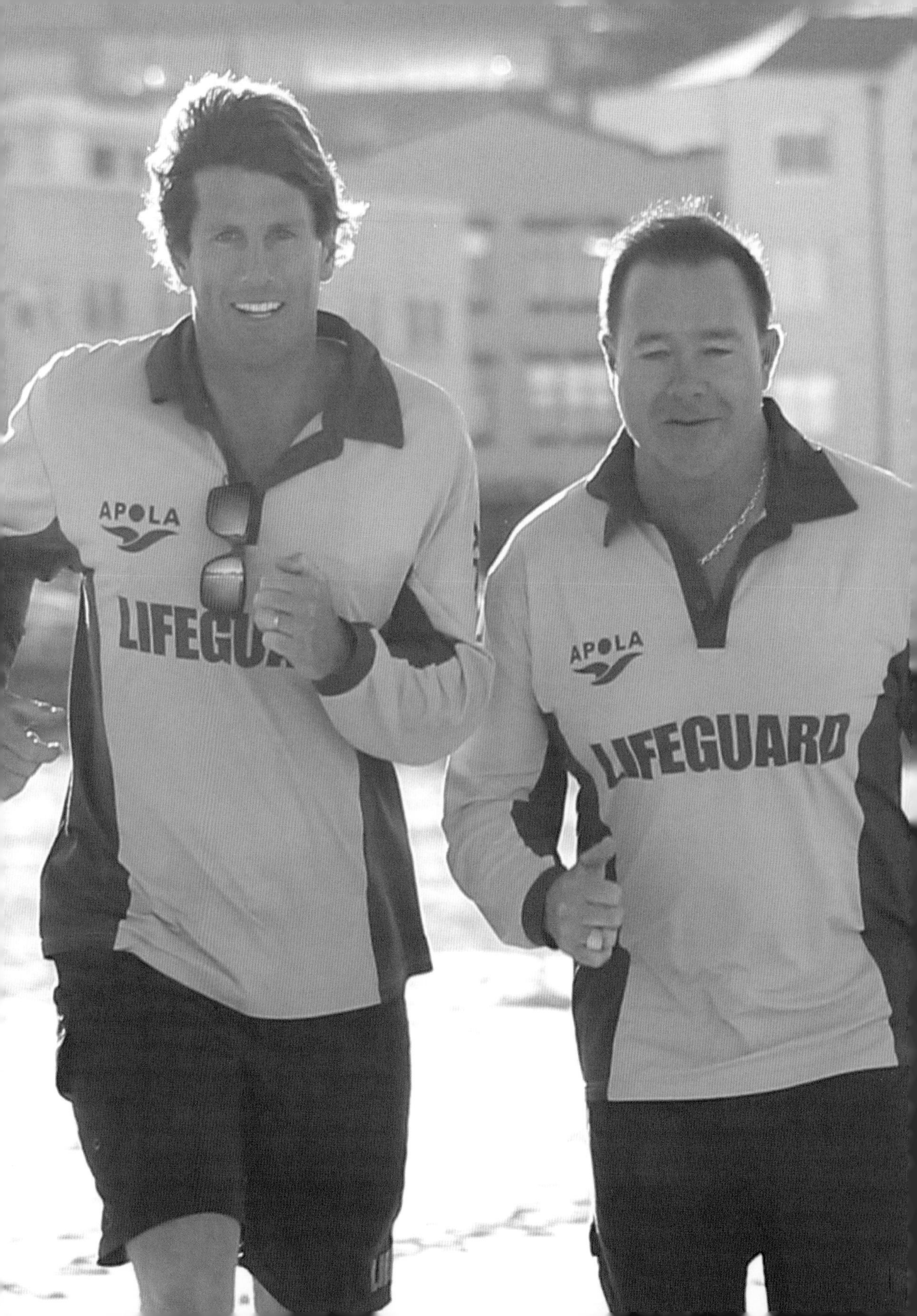
APOLA
LIFEGUARD
APOLA
LIFEGUARD

Why does someone jump off the rocks in massive surf in a clearly dangerous situation to go snorkelling when they are not a strong swimmer? Kerrbox has learnt to see that a lot of things people do don't make sense.

'Another thing I really do hate is watching people doing cartwheels and somersaults off the promenade onto the sand, or running down into the ocean and somersaulting into the water. It sounds like fun, but I have seen so many spinal injuries from people doing stupid things like that. It's such a tragedy when people become quadriplegic from doing something that they love while they are having a holiday. I watched a guy once doing a backflip off the railings on the promenade onto the beach and the next minute he was being carted off with a neckbrace in the ambulance with a spinal injury. It's really stupid. It's just people showing off.'

'We often have to treat people when that happens, so a lot of the time I do yell out and tell people, "Stop doing that – you're going to hurt yourself." We have had some bad spinal injuries here and I hate to see someone's life being taken like that. I don't always have time to do it but it's something I try and stop.'

KERRBOX: 'TIME TO CALL FOR BACK UP!'

The sheer numbers of people on the beach at Bondi means that the lifeguards sometimes have to call on the local Bondi police to help out with crowd control.

'We work with the cops here a lot,' says Kerrbox. 'I get on really well with them. I make a real effort to work with them – especially in my position here as a supervisor. I want to make sure that when we call them they come here first as things can get ugly and nasty here. We like to make them feel welcome in the tower.'

Bondi also attracts its share of people with mental health problems, criminal records, or people who see that the crowds are an opportunity to either run a scam or just steal things.

'We had a guy once who was sexually assaulting women in the surf. We weren't sure at first if that was what was happening so we watched him on the screens in the tower as well as checking it out on the shore – and sure enough we saw him commit an assault, and quite a few women were starting to come up to us and complain about him. So we called the cops before we pulled him out of the water. We had two plain clothes police lined up before we went and asked him to come in with us. Of course he denied it but because we have the cameras on the beach we'd got it on film in the tower to back up the witness statements, so he was charged with aggravated assault.'

Crowd control is a big issue at Bondi, and it's one that the lifeguards have to decide at the time how far they get involved. It's not something they can handle all on their own, and they need to call on back ups in the police or council rangers.

'I always stress to the other guys not to call the police for petty things, if we are always calling them they will get fed up or take it less seriously when we really really need them, like if we need to land a helicopter down here for a medical emergency and we need back up with crowd control to get the chopper down on the grass. The cops also do a lot of undercover operations out of our tower and use our CCTV footage if they need to identify someone or track someone's movements. We will always help them out if they have an emergency as well – which we did once when someone had a heart attack right at the front of their police station up the road. It's taken a long time to develop that relationship and it's one that we really want to keep.'

Kerrbox has been on the team for some time, and has helped Hoppo to build it up. He knows how important it is for the team to have different strengths and be able to work together to complement each other's skills.

'Reidy is always up for a prank. He's also like a frog in a wheelbarrow. You can't keep him still! You know that's not a bad thing, he's a live wire, a glass half full kind of guy. Inside the tower it's a hard job to keep him stuck in there because he wants to be out talking to people and rescuing. His life is like that outside of work too! He is pushbike riding, doing Molakai paddles, chasing chicks, on the radio, organizing charity events. He doesn't stop. I don't know how he does it without falling over. I don't think he sleeps.'

'He's not that keen to be in the tower, he will walk in and say, "How you going fellas?" And in his mind he is already seeing who is where and what's happening. And then he just wants to get out there on the beach, which is good because he knows the lie of the land and what's needing to be done. Watching Reidy is a bit like watching the cartoon character Road Runner you know? You have to check in on him every ten minutes to find out where he is.'

'Maxi is my new tennis partner. We play a lot, but we haven't had a win yet, but we haven't had a loss yet – we've had a draw! I'm always telling him to slow down, even in our tennis match I am telling him to stop a minute and focus. When Maxi first started he would have climbed over barbed wire to get to the action. He was so keen and eager he would drop everything to be where he needed to be. His enthusiasm speaks for itself you know?

'We had a guy once who dropped down with a seizure on the beach right in front of us. So we all went racing down including Maxi and I yelled at him to stop and go back! I needed him to stay in the tower, as we all couldn't go. We can't all be at one place at the same time. We have to take a second, and decide really quickly who is best for the role. We went down and attended to the incident. Maxi was upset at the time when I told him to stop and wait. Then I had to call him down over the radio to bring some equipment. He is one of the fastest amongst us – I mean look at him he is so fit and young and healthy. So it was clear to him that

I needed him – but just in a different way to what he first thought. So he was involved in the incident right up to his ears. A big smile came on his face as he realized he was important to the team, but he had to wait and get instructions sometimes on what that role will be. I have seen a massive change in Maxi as he has learned to assess the situation. Some guys just don't want to go to the really horrific accidents. They will find a way to get out of it if they can. Other guys can deal with it and are the first to get to an incident. That's how Maxi is.'

CHAPTER 13:

Work Hard, Play Hard

Like any job that demands intense dedication, stress, concentration and a huge physical commitment, there has to be a release valve to help the team stay focused and on top of their game. The last thing Hoppo wants is to train lifeguards up, only to have them burn out.

Hoppo has seen several guys leave because they couldn't take the stress and the tragedy, or because of the fear of battling the ocean or being responsible for a difficult rescue. One way he tries to avoid that is to keep up competitiveness between the Bondi Lifeguards, who all want to make sure they are the top or very nearly there.

But he also reckons it's important to have a laugh and let go. There's a strong side to everyone that needs to kick back and see the funny side of life. As Harries says:

'We may be very competitive but when it comes to working together, we are the best mates ever.' So it comes as no surprise that the guys like to play a few pranks now and then, especially on the younger members of the team. There's a golden rule to joking around on the beach – you never make fun of the people you are rescuing, or their family, or the patients that you have to help out. That means the best target for a joke is each other, and then the gloves are off. 'Taking the mickey out of each other is one way to say you're a mate and you are up for it. Yeah, you could say it's a compliment!' says Hoppo.

Maxi is one of the youngest on the team, which makes him pretty easy to target for a prank! It's part of everyone's orientation into the job – it was part of Maxi's traineeship for him to lighten up and realize that there are serious parts of the job but you should also see the funny side of things.

'I don't start jokes,' says Maxi. 'I'm too worried about hurting other people's feelings, and I just don't have that kind of mastermind ability to pull it off. But that's okay because plenty of the other guys do, and they make up for it!'

Kerrbox is a pretty good mastermind. 'I pick on Maxi heaps,' admits Kerrbox. 'He's an easy target!'

When Maxi was a fresh, new recruit on the team aged 16, the guys organized for an ex-heavyweight champion boxer called Big Bob Miravick to come onto the beach and pick a fight with him. Terry McDermott told Maxi to go and tell this guy to get out of the water. Then Bob came back and tried to pick a fight with poor Maxi. 'I was shitting myself,' laughs Maxi. 'I had no idea what do to!'

There's always something that the guys will find funny, even if it is at their own expense. 'One day I was riding the bike', says Maxi, 'And there was a mass of seagulls on the beach, and I was laughing with Kerrbox in the rhino ATV and one of the birds shat straight into my mouth! Can you believe such bad luck! I nearly ran over someone! Another time, I was staying in a mate's flat while he was away and I was looking for somewhere to live. When he was coming back, I cleaned the place from top to bottom –it was spotless. Then the guys came round and trashed the room I was sleeping in, and smashed eggs and tomato sauce all over the roof! So he made out he was furious with me – until I found out that he was in on it as well!'

When it comes to any competitions, or being in the right place at the right time for a rescue, the guys will bust a gut to try and outrun each other to do the best job.

Reidy remembers one time in the tower when Maxi had just started.

'Maxi is always going at the job 110 per cent. He is so keen and quick, sometimes he even beats me, which is saying something! I remember once Maxi answered the phone in the tower. We were all standing there ready for action, looking at him and waiting to see what was going down. We could see by the look on his face that it was something serious.'

'We were waiting for him to finish the call then he just put down the phone, stood up, grabbed some gear and ran out to jump on the jet ski, and just as he opened the door we all yelled, "Hey Maxi what's going on?! What's happened?!" "Oh yeah," He said, "It's someone round the corner (Tamarama), we gotta go!" He's always going 100 miles an hour. It's a good thing. It shows up the other guys who might get a bit lazy.'

REIDY: IT'S LIKE MASH ON TV SOMETIMES

Reidy has a talent for telling funny stories, which stands him in good stead in the radio business. Right now he has some funny stories about Hoppo because they are sharing a flat this year. Reidy has lots of funny stories about Harries as well. 'Is Harries funny, or is it just that he think's he's funny? Some people say he doesn't make sense a lot of the time. But when you stop and take ten minutes and work it out it actually does make sense you know, in a way?'

Reidy is like Maxi – he doesn't mind people having a laugh along with him. He explains it like this; 'Hey I was a fat teenager, I have thick skin – I can cop anything now!'

'One time I was in the tower and there was a beautiful girl on the beach who I knew and I was trying to impress her. I think she was Brazilian. The tyres on the Rhino ATV needed some air so I was under the tower pumping up the tyres. There was a guy drifting out a bit out the back that we all had our eye on and I shouted up, "Let me know if I have to go out for that guy."'

'I was half way through pumping up the tyres when the guys called down to me to get down to the water as the guy was calling out for help. I turned the bike around and went down to the beach so fast that when I hit the front break I went straight over the front of it. The board flew out of the rack and I landed in the sand with the board on top of me. I jumped up, grabbed the board, raced into the water and grabbed the guy who was struggling. I brought him back and came out on the beach and the Brazilian girl was just standing there laughing at me. I got a date though, and we went out that night! Sometimes we rescue people and they are laughing as we pull them out of the water. So in that case I feel I can have a joke with them. You know saying things like: "Where are you from? Scotland? Oh how did I know that!" When it's not a serious situation I like keeping the fun going. Sometimes with hot chicks I will say "well, if you want to get on the board then you will have to kiss me" and laugh. I only ever do it when there is no danger.'

'We've played a lot of jokes and we bag each other out and take the piss a lot. Once I put boot polish on the binoculars when Hoppo was on duty and it took him about a minute to figure out what was wrong! Then another day I hid the jet ski and he thought it had been stolen. That was really funny!'

'I reckon I am the one that instigates a lot of pranks – along with Kerrbox. Kerrbox isn't gullible, he's very smart. He is one of the most unassumingly smart blokes I have ever met and I mean that in the nicest possible way! But if he can feel that there is something fun about to happen, and there's something in the air, even if it is at his expense, then he will roll with it. There's been plenty of occasions when we've managed to get our own back on Kerrbox. The rat incident was a doozy, he doesn't like rats! There was one under the tunnel and Harries was chasing him around the tower and he was running fast!

'When you are working with Kerrbox you know it's going to be a great day. It can be hard at work, but it can be easier when you are working with some fun guys like Kerrbox. Work is always hard at Bondi but he makes it easier! It's like MASH on the TV – we take the piss and then suddenly there is a serious situation and we all know our roles. Game on we can do this.'

HARRIES: PAY BACK TIME!

Hoppo remembers Harries and his brother Sean when they were teenagers, coming down to Bondi Beach and Clovelly and causing trouble for the lifeguards. That boyish sense of humour has continued in the tower, with Harries dishing it out and also getting it back! One famous prank stands out, when Kerrbox and Hoppo got Harries back big time.

'I was at the spray tan studio, getting a tan' remembers Harries. 'We are always wearing shirts at work to cover up from the sun, so I went to the spray tan salon and was lying back enjoying it. Hoppo said he was going to get a spray tan as well, at the same time. Unbeknown to me Kerrbox was hiding in the salon. "Mate", said Hoppo, "There's something wrong with the spray tan bottle, so you have to put these goggles on in case it damages your eyes." So I put on the goggles – which meant I couldn't see anything. Turns out Kerrbox is spraying blue dye all over me! It made me look like a smurf! It was very funny! For them! Hoppo reckons it was pay back time for all the time that I pranked him when I was younger. Well I can tell you it took a while for me to wash it off. It wasn't that water soluble!'

'I've paid Kerrbox back a bit. I've given him hell on radio about being burnt so many times by women that he should be a fireman! And I've chased him with a rat round the tower as well – he is so scared of rats, he hated that. The guys also seem to enjoy dressing up for charities or events. One of the biggest pranks is to dress up in girl's clothes. 'Yeah we dress up a lot!' Says Harries, 'I always end up being a woman, I don't know why! I think it's funny to cross dress! Why wouldn't you? I have to say that Hoppo also looks very good in a nurse's outfit!'

Ryan 'Whippet' Clark is one of the lifeguards on Bondi. He used to be on the famous long-running Australian daytime drama, Home and Away, which is filmed on Sydney's northern beaches in Palm Beach, right up the other end of Sydney.

Kerrbox saw this as a potential gag, and asked an English girl to come to the tower and say she was an actress from London. He convinced her to tell Whippet that she was madly in love with him after seeing him on the TV. Whippet fell for it, for a bit! Until Kerrbox showed up in the tower with the girl. Whippet vowed to get Kerrbox back. And he did, big time.

In 2006 Whippet told Kerrbox that Bondi Rescue had gone over really well in Japan, and that he was one of the most popular stars of the show there. Now he had the chance to be on TV in Japan, in a famous commercial advertising a new energy drink. He told Kerrbox they were looking for someone sporty and well known, and they would pay him around $10,000 for one commercial. Kerrbox said, 'I'm in!'

'They got me down onto the beach on a really hot day when it was packed full of people. The whole beach was watching. There were three members of the Japanese "production team" including a translator, and they were using the film crew from the TV show Bondi Rescue to film it because they were already on location.'

'So the 'director' asked me to repeat this Japanese word over and over so I could remember the name of the drink, 'nikano oshiko'. I had to leap off the jet ski and shout it out. Then I had to come running out of the ocean and say things like, "When I need a drink after working hard on the beach I drink nikano oshiko."'

'They worked me all day! Then the director started to say things like, "Actually you are much taller on television than you are in real life". And, "Can you pull your stomach in a bit more?" and, "I need a bit more charisma, I'm actually a bit disappointed in your acting skills."

'I started to get really pissed off and saying to Whippet that I didn't think I could take much more, and Hoppo was telling me to keep calm otherwise I'd lose my money. So I kept going for a while with the director still getting at me, saying things like: "Hey they call you the Mel Gibson of Japan, back home, but I am not seeing that."'

'So they finally said it was okay, and we were done, and at the end of the day we went up into the tower to look at the final take on the computer screen. I hadn't seen that the guys had been laughing behind me the whole time we were filming. So as soon as I saw that I knew they had got me! And then they told me that what I had been saying meant, "I drink cat's piss." I just broke up.'

'My heart dropped and I was completely humiliated. I didn't know whether to laugh or cry! There was a group of Japanese kids from a school, about 40 of them, who had watched. And the next day they were all shouting out, "Hey Kerrbox you drink cats piss!" So yeah, it was very embarrassing and hard to swallow! If you seach #catspiss on Twitter you can still view the filming. Actually I thought the advert was quite good! I was kind of proud of it! But yep, Whippet, you got me! But I know we all like to blow off a bit of steam and playing pranks on each other is one way we do it.'

'One prank we played against Harrison and Maxi was a classic. Harrison was a trainee from New Zealand. Ball games are banned on Bondi Beach, but we saw that Alessandro Del Piero was on the beach, one of the best soccer players in the world who was on the Italian team that won the World Cup in 2006! I think he was here for a promotion with Sydney FC. I recruited one of my friends to come up to the tower and make a complaint about people playing soccer on the beach to make it look genuine. Then we sent Harrison and Maxi to tell him about the rule of no ball games. "If they cause you any grief, just grab the ball from them." I said. This was going to be good – seeing one of them try to take the ball off a player like Del Piero!'

'When the boys got there, Alessandro and his friends all said they would only stop playing if you let us have a penalty shoot out with you! Maxi radioed up to the tower to ask for my permission, and I said, "Ok that's fine, but don't come back here if you lose!" Harrison had never even kicked a ball before in his life, let alone played soccer, so of course his shot at goal was way off. Then del Piero delivered a beautiful curved ball in the top right pocket and everyone was cheering and laughing. Harrison finally got it! He had heard of the World Cup it seems!'

'All the lifeguards joke about Kerrbox and his relationship with animals – he doesn't like them! 'There was one time in the 2013/14 season that I had to go up the storm drain to rescue a seal. At the north end of the beach there is a huge storm drain, and somehow a seal had swam up into it and got stuck. You could hear it moving around and making these weird noises. I hadn't a clue what I was going to do when I got there, but I was nominated to go and deal with it. 'I didn't have a torch, but I started to walk up into the drain and then it got narrower. I don't like animals much, and I really hate rats. I'm no Bear Grylls, put it that way. Anyway, I kept going and then in the dark I could see the seal's eyes, it sensed I was there and started making this screeching noise. Well, I turned and ran as fast as I could to get out of there, and slammed my forehead on one of the blocks of cement on the roof. Hoppo reckons I ran like a hyena. In the end it came out by itself!'

'We are on our toes every day, and we can never let our guard down. But playing pranks on each other is a way to break out of the stress – you can get a bit down sometimes, and lightening the mood up a bit really helps. We are serious about what we do, but a bit of a fun helps release some of the tension.'

HOPPO: 'WHAT GOES AROUND COMES AROUND'

'I don't mind the guys having some fun at work, actually I'm often right in the middle of it! I think it's good for the guys to loosen up, especially if we have had some heavy days, and particularly if we have lost someone, then the team needs something funny to help us all get back up again. I think one of the funniest pranks was the Kerrbox and the Japanese advertisement. It was done really well, and he was in deep, right till the end. They got him hook, line and sinker. When we played it on the TV in the tower and the guys were in the background laughing at him – he suddenly realized what was going on. That was a classic.'

'Kerrbox got me back when Whippet organized a 30-day challenge. I thought it was a good idea – 30 days without carbs or junk food or fat and an increase in our training regime, so we could lose some weight and convert it to muscle. We all committed to it and got weighed in, and Whippet gave us a healthy eating plan and got us to agree to the rules, and the forfeits if we broke them.'

'Half way through the 30 days, we were all missing our pasta and our beers! So when Kerrbox, who hadn't signed up to the challenge, invited us all round to his place for dinner and his table was full of pasta and pizza and beers and party pies, we thought we were at last away from the TV cameras and could have a night off. I should have twigged when I saw a bunch of flowers on the table – Kerrbox never has flowers in his apartment! We didn't realise that he'd put GoPro cameras all round his house, and the flowers were hiding one of the main microphones – so the whole thing was captured on film. He got us a beauty on that one – we all tucked in – and the next day we were all busted for breaking the rules, and the forfeit was cleaning the toilets in the Bondi Beach Pavilion. I had to do it – I couldn't pull rank at that point I was in it as much as anyone else!'

Christmas is incredibly busy on Bondi, but it's also always full of laughs as well, and a classic Maxi prank was something that all the lifeguards still talk about – the Shrunken Turkey incident!

'We have a barbecue out the back that we use sometimes for lunch. We told Maxi that it was his turn to cook the Christmas turkey for us this year. All he had to do was set it up on the barbecue, but we told him to keep an eye on it as they can shrink a bit in the cooking. We put stuffing in the bird to make it look really good and he put it on, and was in the tower working and keeping an eye on it. Then we organized a group of bikini models to come up and say they were down at the beach for a shoot, and wanted to go in the water but were a a bit nervous, and could they have a lifeguard to look after us?'

'So we generously told Maxi he could take on the job, and as he ran off down to the water we called out, "Don't forget about the turkey!" And he called back, "Yeah I'll be back". But of course he forgot all about it. He was in the surf with the girls! He was only 17, let's face it.'

'While he was away, we swapped the turkey for a very small burnt quail that we had cooked up. After about 45 minutes he came running back up the beach, shouting that he'd come to check on the turkey, goes out to the barbecue, opens the lid, sees the tiny burnt quail and freaks out! That sort of thing could happen any time. The pranks are getting better and better, and we always have plenty of people on hand to help out and make it look good!'

'Harries is normally involved in anything funny, unusual or crazy. He's what we call a nut magnet – anyone who is slightly loopy will always find their way to him!. Any time we are going out a night, or travelling, wherever we are they will find him. Some people say that crazy people like white things and they are attracted to his teeth! It takes him a long time to get ready – cream in his hair, cleaning his teeth. He's not growing old graciously!'

CHAPTER 14:

What does the future hold for Bondi lifeguards?

Bondi has a mixture of lifeguards in age and experience – from the youngest trainees who come in aged 18, to the oldest Harry 'H Man' Nightingale at 64, and the combination is incredibly successful. Harry is up there competing in fitness with the best of them and still working solidly all summer. His experience and authority is priceless and his ability to mentor the younger members is valuable on a day-to-day basis.

Hoppo is in his early 40s, and is still the boss of the team. His management style, which encourages each member to achieve in their own way, is part of the success story of the Bondi lifeguards.

It's a tough job, taking its toll on the mind and body. And the guys who don't have permanent positions need to find another job during the winter. This generally leads them into landscaping, building or short-term jobs, but some of the guys are building careers that can work alongside their jobs on the beach. All the Bondi lifeguards have an extremely positive attitude to life, and what lies ahead for them in the future.

WOMEN IN THE TOWER

One of the changes in the last ten years has seen some woman wanting to join the lifeguard service, although Hoppo isn't exactly swamped with applications from females. Nicola Atherton started as a lifeguard in 2013, before that there was Natalie Grace, and Brooke Cassell, and there was also a casual female lifeguard, Sarah Wells, for a time.

'It's not that women can't be lifeguards,' says Hoppo, 'it's just that it will only suit a certain type of woman. Well it only suits a type of person – I mean a lot of guys can't be lifeguards either. There's a range of skills that you have to have, a lot of physical strength, a good technique for getting people out of the water and up onto the board or the back of the jetski. Brooke had a good technique for doing that. You don't have to be big, but you do have to be fit and strong. And let's face it I have seen a lot of guys who don't have a technique and can't get someone onto a board. Women have the same skills at CPR and their ability to deal with emergency situations is the same. I admit it's a male-dominated place in the tower. It's competitive and very blokey. But it does balance things when there's a woman on the team, and its good to have that.'

'Nicola was faced with a really difficult situation when she had only been a lifeguard for about three months. She was in the tower last November when a young Japanese student drowned. The guys were out there trying to rescue two students and they managed to bring one guy in but the other one drowned. Nicola was in the tower on her own liaising with helicopters and ambulances and managing all the communications. She also had to call the family that he was staying with to break the news. She did an amazing job.'

Hoppo is also introducing iPads into the service this year to help with incident reporting – photographs and details can be easily recorded and tracked back later, especially if the police need the information for serious incidents.

MAXI: 'LIFE IS LIKE THE WEATHER!'

Maxi came in at 16, young and keen and bursting for any experience he could get his hands on. He can't believe his luck in landing the best job ever, that saw him get out of fast food kitchens and into the Pacific Ocean at Bondi.

Maxi would like one of the coveted permanent jobs in the Bondi team, and although they're not that easy to get, he is totally committed to being in the service for as long as he can. Already there for seven years, he's interested in developing skills in the leadership style that he has learnt from Hoppo. Then there's that childhood goal of getting into the fire brigade. Who knows when that will become a possibility? He's still so young, and he's a guy with ambition and lots of energy to put behind any path that his career will take.

'I'm only 22 now,' he says. 'I've had a great run so far! But if I was to die tomorrow, I have a quote on my ribs in a tattoo that everybody could read. It says: "Every step leads you down a path to somewhere. The decisions we make about which path to take makes us who we are today. Make it happy and positive". I should have been a philosopher ha ha ha!,' he laughs out loud. 'But seriously, I know that what will help me in the future is the way that I look at life – and I reckon that no matter how bad or angry you get, as long as you're doing what you want to be doing, you're unstoppable. No matter what people say about you, you're not a bad person, and if you believe in what you are doing, you will get there and prove them all wrong. That's what happened to me for sure.'

Where does he get this outlook from? Maxi explained that when he was younger, he had a up close look at what happens to you if you are threatened by health issues and he had a taste of what it could be like to lose his parents, both of whom he loves and is really close to. It's something he also draws on in his opposition to drugs in young kids.

'My mum nearly died of liver failure and the doctors gave her ten years to live when I was younger. That really hit me hard, and I was scared. When I was young she told me to make sure you never take drugs because it will hit your liver. So I have given her that promise. There's a lot of drugs around here in Bondi and the Eastern Suburbs of Sydney. I just made a promise to my family that I wouldn't do that.'

'My dad has always been the provider for my family – he's always been a hard worker and was the only one earning any money while my mum was sick. Then he developed type 2 diabetes and had to take insulin regularly, which is such a drag for him. So I've learnt from what my parents have been through – I really want to try and avoid that, and be as healthy as I can. 'But I'm really happy about my life – I'm lucky. And I think you create your own success. People who sit back and wait for things won't make it happen. Just be yourself and you can accomplish so much – people don't realize that. If you know you're a good person then good things will happen to you. You know what? I really believe that.'

'I think my philosophy makes me pretty unique and different amongst people my age. I mean everyone has a laugh and bags people out and people annoy you – but I try and deal with that differently because I just think there is so much negativity already out there. And jealousy. I've copped that a bit of that from people already especially after the TV show.'

'Lots of people say to me that they think that I'm just a young guy having a good time – as if this isn't hard work! I'd like to see them out there paddling over massive waves and bringing people in all day.'

'I'm a kid from a working class family. I've seen people being bullied and I've seen its effects on people. I've seen what bullying can do to someone's self esteem, and how it can really have a negative impact on them when they grow up. A lot of the suicides that we get here are from people who haven't been able to cope with the negativity in their lives. The message I have for

the bullies out there is this. Everyone is in a different situation. And you should realize that – you don't want to have someone's suicide on your conscience.'

REIDY: 'YOU MAKE YOUR OWN CHOICES.'

The team swells in the summer and there is lots of work, but in the winter the work falls off. Because of that, Reidy is always busy and on the look out for ways to develop other things in business or in the media in the winter.

'In the winter I don't have any work here at the beach,' he says, 'But actually I'm okay with that, I'm developing lots of other things as well. A few of us have started a Bondi Rescue clothing business. I'm helping with that and I'm also running a CPR and emergency training business.'

Reidy is always looking to find how they can work better at Bondi as well, and deliver a better service to the public. He's involved in a group looking at an app for mobile phones that they can use at work, so they can record incidents and build up the data about the events surrounding it.

Despite being followed by live TV cameras all day while the Bondi Rescue TV show is being created, it is radio that Reidy loves. Together with Maxi he is already releasing life podcasts on their Meat in the Sandwhich brand and learning how to be a panel operator in a radio studio.

'I'd love to work in radio some more. I can talk to anyone and I love talking to people! I wrote to a lot of people and got a lot of knockbacks when I first started trying to get into radio. All my mates said learn how to operate the panel – that way you can get into the studio and learn how it all works. Well what I have learnt is that pannelling is hard! Give me ten people drowning in a rip any day – that's easy in comparison!'

Reidy wrote to one of Sydney's top shock jocks, Alan Jones, and, 'Alan's producer called me and said I could come in and give it a go. So I go in regularly and learn from the professionals.

A lot of the guys there have all sorts of qualifications, they've been to university for three years and studied sound engineering, but I didn't let that get in the way. I said that's fine. So I have been paneling for a few announcers – not the big guys – but some of the smaller ones. I'm going to be doing a six-week shift soon. I'm also recording weekly podcasts with Maxi. We started out interviewing lifeguards and we get about 500 downloads. We look at things coming up, our take on what's happening in Bondi, do fun interviews. We meet lots of celebrities – presenter James Tobin, actor Dan McPherson for example – and get them in for an interview. And we include all sorts of information – some fitness tips, how to prepare for fun runs how to prepare for marathons. Stuff like that.'

'We called it The Meat in the Sandwich, and we got an illustrator to draw us in between two pieces of bread. Podcasts are great because you can listen to them whenever you like. I would love to have my own radio station.'

'I've got lots of other plans and ideas as well. I'm planning to put on a run-swim-run event here at Bondi to raise money for the local youth centre. They have basketball courts and they are great for kids to go to. They really helped me when I was in high school and hanging around and looking for something to do. I think youth centres are really great things in a community.'

Reidy has been through lots of different stages in his life – from the fat teenage boy who was bullied, to the uncertain guy juggling work as a garbo and lifeguard, to the TV personality lifeguard pursuing all sorts of different businesses.

'My life is amazing now. It wasn't always like this though! So my message to everyone is – inspire yourself. It's never too late to change. Things haven't always gone to plan for me but if I can change my life, you can too.'

BONDI LIFEGUARDS NEVER GIVE UP!

Harries says he also never saw what shape his life was going to take. He has always been a ladies man but now all of that may be a thing of the past, as recently his life has changed, in the shape of a woman called Emily, and a little boy called Billie.

'I had a girlfriend on and off for about seven years. But it didn't work out. I look back and see a lot of the problems were my fault, but you learn a lot as you go along. Then I went on a blind date. One of my Ironman friends, champion Leon Hay, was going out with his girlfriend and asked me to come along. At first I said no, I know it's going to end dismally! But then I had second thoughts and went along. So we met for dinner and I looked across at her and she was stunning and beautiful – in every way – she was smart and she was elegant and so soft. And all my past seemed to melt away! The problem for me was that I had to go to the Maldives the next day for a surfing magazine photoshoot! They had set up a photoshoot with me and lots of girls – they were also looking for some sort of background story as they knew I would probably be in the bunk room sooner or later! So I'm there at this shoot telling all these girls in bikinis that I had met a girl and fallen in love with her!'

'Then I came back and met up again with Emily and history was created. We got married in 2012, and I am such a lucky man to have found someone so beautiful and intelligent to have in my life. We now have our six month old baby boy, Billie. Being a Dad is the greatest thing I have ever done – apart from marrying my wife of course! I want Billie to look up to me and I'm thinking of what the future holds. I want him to work hard and achieve whatever he can.'

'I've got quite a few ideas about my future as well. I'm doing my Pilates diploma and I would like to run a health centre. Imagine that! There would be lycra everywhere! I'm still doing competitions as well, in Longboard I have won it three times. Is it enough? No! I reckon I have another three Australian titles in me.'

'I'm also going to be a lifeguard for as long as I can. My heart is in the lifeguards. I really want to give a lot back. I always want to be part of some sort of action – disasters – something big going down. That's when I lower my heart rate the best. I can drag myself out of my body and remain calm and collected.'

Kerrbox also says that his life motto is to never give up, and enjoy life as much as you can. 'You never know when it could be your last day!' He says.

'It's too easy to give up,' says Harries. 'People keep saying I can't do this and I can't do that. It's up to you – how much do you want to be an Australian champion? When I rock up to that starting line at any competition and I look across to the other competitors I ask myself – are they talented? Yes they are. Have they been out in the surf? Not as much as me. I want to win and keep that burning flame inside!'

Hoppo has the same drive and commitment to life's possibilities: he says that if you have a passion don't give up on it!

'You don't know where you are going to end up or where you're going to use that passion! Plenty of times I have sat there thinking that things weren't going to happen for me – the TV show and the new business and our life opportunities are not going to happen. But I always knew there was something that I could give back to people – and that I had something bigger and better to give in my life. I knew that lifeguarding was one thing – but there was more to me than that. So the show and my business have made me realize that. Chase your dreams. It might take 40 years but you will get there in the end. No matter what it is. Stay positive.'

Being a lifeguard means relying on your body to stay fit. Hoppo was challenged this year by an eye operation he had to have.

'In about May last year I started to notice a sort of curtain growing over my eye so I went to the doctor and he said you have a detached retina. I was rushed into hospital for an operation and after I came out, it meant I had to lie down for about five days. I was in a lot of pain, but I couldn't' do much about it.'

'Harries, Dean and Kerrbox were running things while I was away and it was winter – so I wasn't too worried. But it made me start thinking about what I was going to do in the future. So I started to think about business ideas and plans for several of us in the team with our Bondi Lifeguard clothing business.'

The operation was a success and Hoppo says he was lucky that he caught it at that time. 'Things like this make you stronger as a person,' he says. Hoppo is also a proud Dad with two young teenage daughters. He was really happy when his eldest daughter said to him one day: 'A lot of people don't think there are heroes in real life, but they haven't met my dad.'

'She's making a lot of the right decisions now as a teenager.' Says Hoppo proudly. 'I'm pretty open with her and talk to her about issues so I'm confident she's going to be fine.'

Never one to let someone else have the last say, Harries says that his message to all the Bondi Rescue fans is simple:

'You are all firstly so adorable for taking time to watch a bunch of beach bums! You're amazing. The messages we receive are amazing. You can see our camaraderie and friendship and how far we go to help our mates out. We really appreciate all your support and we love your messages. So I guess what we'd all like to say is – Thanks!'

Safety on the beach

The Bondi Lifeguards' message to everyone who comes to Bondi is to follow these simple rules to be safe at the beach:

- Always swim between the red and yellow flags, never swim outside them.

- Do not swim directly after a meal or if under the influence of alcohol or drugs.

- Only swim when the red and yellow flags are flying. If there are no flags, the beach is closed or unpatrolled.

- Do not panic if caught in a current or undertow. Raise one arm into the air to signal for lifeguard assistance. Float until help arrives.

- Do not struggle if seized with a cramp. Raise your arm for help and float. Keep the part of your body that is cramping perfectly still.

- Do not swim if unsure of surf conditions. Always seek the advice of a lifeguard or lifesaver.

- Do not struggle against a rip or current. Swim diagonally across it.

Biographies

TRENT "MAXI" MAXWELL

Trent Maxwell AKA "Maxi" grew up surfing on Maroubra Beach. Joining the Bondi Lifeguards when he was 16, in 2007, Maxi was the youngest lifeguard the team took onboard. This 2013 Cleo Bachelor takes a keen interest in helping the community, keeping fit, surfing, travelling and generally enjoying life. Maxi's passion lies in helping those fighting depression and suicide (he completed a 3500km jet skiing mission from Sydney to Cairns to raise awareness for Australia's National Youth Mental Health Foundation, headspace). You can find him on:

Twitter: @lifeguardmaxi

Facebook: trent.m.maxwell

Instagram: @lifeguardbox

ANDREW "REIDY" REID

Growing up surfing at Maroubra and Bronte Beach, Andrew Reid AKA "Reidy" has worked as a Bondi Lifeguard for over 12 years and knows the ocean like the back of his hand, helping save hundreds of lives over the years. Reidy has a keen interest in charities concerned with youth care and building awareness for youth centres in Australia. Reidy is one of the fittest lifeguards on Bondi beach, often competing in marathons and successfully competing in Ironman Triathlons (finishing in 9 hours 24 minutes). Reidy loves making podcasts, learning how to panel in a radio studio, competing and keeping fit, surfing and travelling. You can find him on:

Twitter: @Reidy__

Facebook: BondiRescueReidy

Instagram: @reidy__

ANTHONY "HARRIES" CARROLL

Growing up surfing at Clovelly Beach, Anthony Carroll AKA "Harries", has been lifeguarding for over 18 years and has now joined the Bondi Rescue lifeguard team. Harries takes interest in charities about youth care and Westmead Hospital. Harries is an all time family man, loving husband and father. In his spare time, Harries likes to try and teach his baby how to swim, competing and keeping fit. With over 3000 rescues under his belt, this former Cleo Bachelor of the Year is a true Bondi hero. You can find him on:

Twitter: @LG_Harries

Facebook: anthony.carroll.9843

Instagram: @harriescarroll

BRUCE "HOPPO" HOPKINS

Bruce Hopkins AKA "Hoppo" has been working as a lifeguard with Waverley Council, which oversees Bondi, Tamarama and Bronte Beaches, since 1991. He was appointed head lifeguard in 2000 and is one of the longest serving and most experienced lifeguards on the roster. Hoppo is a multi-award winning lifeguard taking out the Australian Lifeguard of the year award in 2006, and 2 x Gold medals at the Australian Surf Lifesaving titles in the Double Ski and the Board Paddle in 2008. With 23 years of lifeguarding experience, Hoppo has been involved in more resuscitations than any other lifeguard in the service. You can find him on:

Twitter: @lifeguardhoppo

Facebook: bruce.hopkins

Instagram: lifeguardhoppo

ROD "KERRBOX" KERR

Rod Kerr AKA "Kerrbox" has been a Bondi lifeguard for 20 years. With over 10 years experience as a pro surfer and placing 6th during the World Surfing Tour in the early 90s, Kerrbox is no stranger to the waves. Growing up alongside fellow lifeguard Hoppo, Kerrbox has just fewer than 40 revivals under his belt and is passionate about helping others and saving lives. Kerrbox has keen interests in charities concerned with the Schizophrenia Research Institute, Randwick Children's Hospital and is currently working alongside LivetoGive, an organisation that coordinates community projects to support disadvantaged children in the community. You can find him on:

Twitter: @lifeguardbox

Facebook: rod.kerr.14

Instagram: @lifeguardbox

References

Based on interviews conducted between 20 June and 17 July 2014.

Online sources:

http://www.theaustralian.com.au

http://www.abc.net.au

http://www.aquabumps.com/2009/02/13/shark-attack-at-bondi/

http://tenplay.com.au/channel-ten/bondi-rescue/about

http://www.waverley.nsw.gov.au/recreation/visitors/my_bondi_summer

http://www.apola.asn.au/safety.htm

http://en.wikipedia.org/wiki/History_of_surfing

http://www.migrationheritage.nsw.gov.au/exhibition/objectsthroughtime/surfboard/

http://www.surfresearch.com.au/

First published in 2015 by New Holland Publishers Pty Ltd
London • Sydney • Auckland

The Chandlery Unit 9 50 Westminster Bridge Road London SE1 7QY United Kingdom
1/66 Gibbes Street Chatswood NSW 2067 Australia
218 Lake Road Northcote Auckland New Zealand

www.newhollandpublishers.com

A record of this book is held at the British Library and the National Library of Australia.

ISBN 9781742576008

Managing Director: Fiona Schultz
Project Editor: Joanne Rippin/Holly Willsher
Designer: Andrew Quinlan
Photographs: Robb Cox
Production Director: Olga Dementiev
Printer: Toppan Leefung Printing Ltd

10 9 8 7 6 5 4 3 2 1

Keep up with New Holland Publishers on Facebook
www.facebook.com/NewHollandPublishers